Alicia Edwards

111 Places for Kids in London That You Shouldn't Miss

111

T0243720

emons:

Coverdesign: Karolin Meinert
Layout: Editorial Design & Artdirection, Conny Laue,
based on a design by Lübbeke | Naumann | Thoben and Nina Schäfer
Maps: altancicek.design, www.altancicek.de
Basic cartographical information from Openstreetmap,
© OpenStreetMap-Mitwirkende, OdbL
Edited by: Ros Horton
Printing and binding: Grafisches Centrum Cuno, Calbe
Printed in Germany 2024
ISBN 978-3-7408-2196-8
First edition

Guidebooks for Locals & Experienced Travellers
Join us in uncovering new places around the world at
www.111places.com

FOREWORD

Every day feels like a new day of discovery in London. One of the most diverse cities in the world, it is draped in fascinating history, iconic landmarks, pioneering architecture, multicultural cuisines, stunning green spaces, and urban housing lived in by people from all walks of life. It is a place where everyone is welcome. This great city is constantly changing, and being part of it makes you feel truly alive! Writing this book has been a wonderful journey, though shortlisting 111 places (from my original list of over 300!) was challenging to say the least. Every location seemed deserving of inclusion, but I've crafted a varied list to introduce families to new parts of the capital that you can explore together.

My daughter accompanied me when I visited many of the places featured in this book, so if it got a thumbs up, it was listed! Personally, I loved heading out of my Zone 1 bubble and really getting to know Outer London better. What was surprising was just how close everything actually is… Zone 6 always seemed a long haul to me. But now that I have a taste for it, we'll be venturing out a lot more to see what each of the boroughs has to offer.

Exploring London with a child and their boundless curiosity is super fun. In a city so diverse we uncovered a multitude of hidden gems. My daughter's constant wonder and joy at experiencing and learning with each trip was wonderful to witness, and let's face it, I've learned a lot too. I am by no means a historian, professional photographer or expert in anything, but I am a mother from London. Hopefully that's enough for you to trust my guidance and head out to make some of your own memories together in this amazing city.

111 PLACES

1_ALL HALLOWS CHURCH

The tower that 'moved'

Standing tall on a main thoroughfare between Richmond and Twickenham, All Hallows Church may have previously taken this route itself. Originally based on Lombard Street in the City of London, the church and its square bell tower dominated the local skyline. But it was taken down stone by stone and, along with all its furnishings, was reassembled right here. Many people walk past the church daily, have parties, weddings, and piano lessons in and around the church but have no idea that it has only been in this location since 1940.

During the Reformation (a new division of Christianity called Protestantism that swept through Europe in the 16th century) many of London's churches suffered. Religious art, statues and decorative sculptures were hidden or destroyed as it was thought that plain churches were more suitable than highly decorated ones. In the 1920s, many of Sir Christopher Wren's London churches were destroyed. One of his churches marked for destruction was All Hallows Church.

So how did the church come to arrive on Chertsey Road in Twickenham? As the population in the suburbs grew, churches were needed, and therefore it was decided to save All Hallows from destruction and relocate it for use by a new community. On 9 November, 1940 the then Bishop of London, whose predecessor had laid the first foundation stone in July of 1939, dedicated the church, and was quoted saying 'We all thought it was marvellous that the bells which rang out over the City of London would now ring out here'.

TIP: Twickenham Stadium, home to England rugby, has a great atmosphere on match days, especially during the Six Nations. You can also watch rugby union matches: check the website for fixtures.

Address 138 Chertsey Road, Twickenham, TW1 1EW, +44 (0)208 241 2345, www.allhallowstwick.org.uk // Getting there Train to Twickenham // Hours Viewable from the outside 24 hours; check website for visiting times // Ages 4+

2_ALL STAR LANES

Skittles and shakes

Located in a quiet Holborn side street via a basement entrance, you'll find All Star Lanes, a hidden gem for a good time. Inside you'll be greeted at reception by helpful staff to check you in. So what activities are on offer? Well, let's start with changing your shoes. Yep, if you opt for bowling you'll need to swap your footwear for some suave bowling shoes and get ready to strike. If you aren't very good at bowling (kids or adults can have the bumpers if needed), or maybe it's not really your thing, fear not because All Star Lanes has more to offer than just tenpins.

Whether you can sing or not, it doesn't matter here as you'll be comfortably boxed away in a private karaoke room where you can sing or screech to your heart's desire to one of the thousands of songs up for selection. To keep those vocal cords hydrated you can order drinks to the room, or hold off until the session is over.

After all that singing and bowling you can refuel in the American-style diner with a milkshake and burger. If you are wearing white, avoid the Dirty Dawg or be shameless and bib it up! There's a kids' menu on offer too. In fact, they even offer family package deals to induce bowling and food as well as teen packages (ages 11–17 years) and kids' parties. If you wanted to put on the ultimate party, there is a private room with two bowling lanes called 'The Lodge', which is perfect for larger families and occasions. Children are allowed in the venue until 6pm daily, so be sure to book in advance.

Address Victoria House, Bloomsbury Place, London, WC1B 4DA, www.allstarlanes.co.uk // Getting there Tube to Holborn (Piccadilly and Central Lines) // Hours Check website for hours // Ages 5+

3_ ARCHES OF LONDON BRIDGE

When it all fell down, where did the arches go?

For centuries, London Bridge was the only crossing over the River Thames. Its style and engineering have developed hugely over the years. While today the bridge stands strong, made of materials robust enough to hold the weight of multiple London buses, its original build was more modest. Back in A.D. 50 the Romans erected the first London Bridge using wooden planks laid across anchored boats. Crossing that seems more like a challenge for a TV show than a commuting bridge in the centre of the capital!

After being rebuilt as a fixed bridge in 984, it wasn't to last long. In 1014, London fell under the attack of Viking invaders who destroyed the bridge. Over the years, London Bridge was rebuilt several times due to damage and fire, and at one point it started to sink due to the weight of shops and dwellings built along it. More disturbingly, for a time the heads of traitors were displayed on spikes along the bridge. This practice went on for many years until King Charles II claimed the throne and got rid of this morbid display. Thanks, Chas!

So where are the arches of one of the previous iterations of London Bridge? In Victoria Park you'll find two 10-foot-tall arches that were moved there in 1860. Have you heard the rhyme *London Bridge is Falling Down*? Some say it's referring to the Viking invasion, while others say it relates to the bridge being knocked down and rebuilt in 1831. Whatever the origin of the rhyme, have a seat in the old arch in Victoria Park and sing the merry tune.

Address Victoria Park Road, Bow, London, E9 5EQ // Getting there Overground to Hackney Wick // Hours Daily 7am – dusk // Ages 0+

TIP: Victoria Park makes for a nice walk with the pram and little ones.

4_BABYLON PARK

Ride an indoor rollercoaster

While the hopes for turning Battersea Power Station into a London-based theme park weren't quite realised, thrill seekers and amusement lovers can head to Camden to ride London's only indoor rollercoaster!

Set against a backdrop of neon lights and creatures from outer space, Babylon Park is the ultimate play zone. As soon as you enter this underground amusement galaxy, you are greeted by friendly looking green aliens, fluorescent multicoloured lights and zany buzzing and beeping sounds bursting from the games machines that transport you straight back to your own childhood.

As well as the rollercoaster, other rides include a spinning musical ride, a drop tower, bumper cars, a miniature alien wheel ride, plus traditional funfair games such as Creature Catch (like hook a duck except it's a unicorn/duck interbreed!) and ring toss. You can also have a go on the VR simulator, which takes you into another galaxy and beyond! As with many amusements, you collect tickets and can exchange them for prizes. Games are suitable for players all the way from tiny tots to teens (and their parents too of course). They also offer SEN mornings for neurodivergent children and their families. If you need to boost your energy after all of the excitement, head to their restaurant to refuel.

Babylon Park offers extreme joy all year round, but especially during the colder and wetter months. Plan to be here for a few hours as time really does fly when you are whizzing around another universe!

Address 8 Castlehaven Road, London, NW1 8QU, +44 (0)208 819 0044, www.babylonpark.com // Getting there Tube to Camden Town (Northern Line) // Hours Mon–Fri noon–8pm, Sat 10am–10pm, Sun 10am–9pm // Ages 5+

TIP: Explore Camden High Street and the surrounding markets for shops and stalls selling goods of all kinds.

5_ BARKING PARK

A mystical unicorn lake

Housing three fantastic family-friendly attractions, Barking Park is definitely one to visit, especially in the summer months. First up is Barking Splash Park, the biggest splash park in London. Water sparkles as it hits the sunlight after bursting up into the air before cascading down onto joyous children. Staff are on hand to entertain the kids, and the mascot, Splashy, can be seen having a boogie too. For added thrills, kids can have a go in the Walk-on-Water balls (like giant bubbles on water) or race on the mini pedal boats. Sessions are timed and the park is enclosed so it doesn't get too busy at peak times.

After a splash, head over to the UK's only unicorn lake. It's a unique sight to observe countless colourful mythical creatures floating along the shimmering water. Each unicorn has a cutesy name such as Cookie, Giggle, Rainbow, Magic and Henry of course. Up to five riders can fit on each boat – sorry, unicorn – so round up your party and dress as colourfully as you can for this magical experience.

Now you've been in the water, then on the water, how about some bouncing to fully dry off? Bounsea boasts nearly 600 square yards of energetic, colourful amusement! There's a baby zone for the youngest bouncer and, luckily for us, there is no top age limit. With slides, climbing walls and a challenge track, it sure makes working out a lot more exciting than the gym! You can make a day of it at Barking Park and visit all three attractions (there are multi attraction deals on tickets).

TIP: 'I'm hungry' is what you'll hear after all that energy burning. To refuel, head into Barking for a selection of cuisines including Turkish, African, Portuguese, American and more…

Address Barking Park, Longbridge Road, Essex, IG11 8TA, www.splashparkbarking.co.uk // Getting there Overground or tube to Barking (District and Hammersmith & City Lines) // Hours Hours differ, so check website for each attraction // Ages Splash Park 0+, Unicorns 1+, Bounsea 1+

6_ BATTERSEA POWER STATION

They'll need a huge chimney sweep!

London's skyline is recognisable worldwide, with internationally known buildings including St Paul's Cathedral, the Shard, Big Ben, The Gherkin and the iconic Battersea Power Station.

Once a key contributor to the UK's industry, generating power to a fifth of London, Battersea Power Station is a well-loved landmark for many, but this hasn't always been the case. In the 1960s it was dubbed a pollution monster, emitting smoke and a wretched smell, which deterred the public from visiting the surrounding areas, including the beauty of Battersea Park just next door.

Designed by architect Sir Giles Gilbert Scott who also designed Bankside Power Station (now the Tate Modern), Battersea Power Station became a symbolic icon of London, even featuring on Pink Floyd's *Animals* album cover. The Power Station was decommissioned in 1983, and later sold to John Broome, the then owner of Alton Towers, who aspired to turn the disused building into a theme park for London. This didn't quite work out, though it would have been hugely popular and saved thrill seekers a journey out of London to get their adrenaline pumping!

After much painstaking redevelopment, Battersea Power Station is now open to the public, and a hub of history, modern living, culture and fun! Families can enjoy dining, indoor activities, seasonal installations, ice skating in winter, outdoor summer activities and best of all a unique chimney lift experience, Lift 109, where you can enjoy a spectacular 360-degree view of London.

FUN

TIP: Can you see Albert Bridge? What is banned from this bridge as it could make the bridge fall down? Marching! Although allowed to cross the bridge, soldiers must break step when trooping across it!

Address Battersea Power Station, Nine Elms, London, SW11 8EZ, www.batterseapowerstation.co.uk // **Getting there** Tube to Battersea Power Station (Northern Line) // **Hours** Shops open Mon–Sat 10am–8pm, Sun noon–6pm; cafés and Lift 109 often open earlier and later // **Ages** 0+

7_THE BLUE HOUSE

A cardboard cut-out dwelling

In the back streets of Bethnal Green, nestled in among old London brown brick buildings, you will find a burst of postmodern pop art style living. In days gone by, this area was a busy thoroughfare for those taking livestock into the City. Many original terraced buildings varying from the two-storey Regency design to the later three-storey Victorian style still remain. However, there is one house that stands out from the crowd.

Completed in 2002, but way ahead of its time, The Blue House combines a home and office, which is perfect for the post pandemic craving to work closer to home now desired by the masses. This commute couldn't get any shorter! The building also houses a roof terrace with views over London's roof tops. Looking at the house from the curb side of an old Hackney Street evokes a bizarre sensation of real world mixed with imagination, so much so that the building has become labelled as one of the most important houses built in modern times. Originally designed by renowned architect Sean Griffiths, this creation was included in The *Guardian*'s 25 most important buildings of the 21st century. Across London, architects design statement buildings incorporating colour and playfulness in an otherwise grey surrounding. Admire Will Alsop's magnificent design for Peckham Library, and Renzo Piano's vibrant 14-storey build that towers over St Giles-in-the-Fields.

TIP: Hackney City Farm is just around the corner. There you'll find animals, activities and a shop selling organic produce.

Take a look at The Blue House's nod to a comic book style and the cardboard cut-out feel. Can you design something similar?

Address 2 Garner Street, London, E2 9AQ // Getting there Overground to Cambridge Heath // Hours Viewable from the outside only // Ages 5+

8_THE BMX TRACK LONDON

Become a world champion!

Burgess Park ticks a lot of boxes when it comes to outdoor activities. If you are a fishing fan, head to the lake. Love flowers? Check out Chumleigh World Gardens. Rugby, tennis, football, cricket, climbing – it would be hard to find yourself with nothing to do here.

During the summer, children can enjoy playing in the water jets. For the running enthusiast, the park offers a three-mile running route around the perimeter marked with butterfly symbols on the pathway. On top of all of that, it's also the home of the Peckham BMX Club. Here you can hire a BMX bike (if you don't have one) and learn some skills. Whether you are a beginner on a balance bike, or a whizz on wheels, there's plenty of space. You don't even have to book, as they have weekly scheduled 'rock up and ride' sessions.

Peckham BMX Club London started in 2004 and was headed up by Radio DJ and TV Presenter Ck Flash alongside Southwark Council and Edwardes Cycles. It started with just four kids and now has over 150 members! Since 2004, the club has shaped world champions and continues to fashion these skills and spread the enthusiasm and passion to hundreds of young riders every month. The floodlit BMX track is really well maintained and it's great to see that they cater for children as young as two years old. For those keen to get out onto the open track, the minimum age is eight years. The club prides itself on inclusivity, offering sessions for people with learning disabilities, autism and sensory needs.

It's *wheelie* good!

TIP: Take a walk over the 'Bridge to Nowhere' in Burgess Park.

Address Wells Way, London, SE5 0PX, +44 (0)207 703 5936, www.southwark.gov.uk // Getting there Tube to Oval (Northern Line) // Hours Park open 8am–6pm; BMX Track London open daily to 9pm // Ages 2+

9_BOW STREET POLICE MUSEUM

The OG Police Force

Have you ever heard of the Bow Street Runners? They were London's original law enforcement service that was founded in 1749 and had only a team of six men. Working for Henry Fielding, who set up the force from the Bow Street Magistrates' Court, the Bow Street Runners travelled nationwide to detain criminals. By 1800 there were 68 of them, then in 1839 they merged with the Metropolitan Police, which had been formed 10 years earlier. They turned out to be very effective – crime fell and conviction rates increased.

On the site of the original Bow Street Magistrates' Court, The Bow Street Police Museum is a small but perfectly formed museum that tells the story of the Bow Street Runners and the Metropolitan Police officers who followed in their footsteps. Not only will you learn of the fascinating tales of Bow Street and its distinctive links with police history, you can even sit in the old police cells and imagine what it was like to be locked up over 100 years ago! It's full of fascinating equipment and the possessions of Bow Street officers – like beat books, truncheons and handcuffs.

The museum offers an array of guided walks, private tours and evening talks along with a fantastic line up of family activities throughout the year. One of our favourite family activities was the fingerprint workshop where we got inked up to have our fingerprints taken and learn the history of fingerprint forensics. We even got to take home a police style fingerprint card as a keepsake. It was very interesting indeed!

Address 28 Bow Street, Martlett Court, London, WC2E 7AW, www.bowstreetpolicemuseum.org.uk // Getting there Tube to Covent Garden (Piccadilly Line) // Hours Fri – Sun 11am – 4.30pm (Last entry 4pm) // Ages 6+

BOW STREET
POLICE
MUSEUM

TIP: The Garden Cinema
is an exquisite independent
cinema that screens family films
throughout the year. They show
all the old classics from *Bambi*
to *Home Alone*.

10_BRIXTON WINDMILL

A windmill in London?

You may envisage a windmill standing tall in the countryside surrounded by the fields and trees of Britain's green and pleasant land, but did you know that there is actually a windmill in Zone 2? Head to Windmill Gardens in Brixton Hill to see this wonderfully restored working mill, originally built in 1816.

Brixton Windmill is bursting with history, having started life as a mill producing wholemeal flour back in the days when Brixton was open land. In 1862 the mill closed and the reason seems obvious when you know. What does a windmill need in order to work efficiently?

Wind! A windmill needs wind! However, in the 1850s London's centre was spreading ever wider, so the erection of new housing and taller buildings created a wind block, thus stopping the sails from operating the mill. Years later, the owner decided to return to the mill, and installed new engineering resulting in a steam- and later gas-powered windmill, and the return of flour milling. Due to mass production from rival companies, the mill closed in 1934 and remained derelict until London County Council acquired it and surrounding land.

After a few more closures and restorations, Brixton Windmill reopened to the public in 2011, and even more thrilling in 2014 the mill began producing flour again. You can pick up a bag of Brixton Windmill flour to take home with you. They also offer a range of activities and events throughout the year from family baking (no guesses which flour they use) to a Beer and Bread festival.

Address Windmill Gardens, 100 Blenheim Gardens, Brixton Hill, London, SW2 5DA, www.brixtonwindmill.org // Getting there Tube or train to Brixton (Victoria Line) // Hours Tours Mar–Oct 2nd weekend of every month, but see website to plan your visit (booking recommended) // Ages 4+

TIP: Take a wander around Brixton village market for a truly diverse and vibrant shopping and dining experience.

11_ BRODIE ROAD POST BOX

Who reigns?

It's hard to walk through a town or residential area and not pass a post box. Dotted around the country these vibrant red pillars are an icon of the UK and an important part of our communication throughout the years. You may have also seen a gold post box on your travels, representing the London 2012 Olympics, and athletes who took part. In Marston you'll find an 'NHS blue' post box installed to celebrate Captain Sir Thomas Moore's 100th birthday and his fundraising for the NHS during the COVID-19 pandemic. In Rochester you'll find a post box set in a wall, which was used by Charles Dickens to correspond with his publishers, editors and friends.

You may also notice a wonderful trend of post box toppers. Groups across the country create crochet toppers to mark special events such as King Charles III's coronation. It's not just the big events: toppers come in all styles, celebrating the local area, seasons, sports and more. The variety is endless.

What makes the post box on Brodie Road so special? It's one of 161 red pillar post boxes commissioned during the short reign of King Edward VIII before he penned his abdication letter. Look at the letters E VIII R. They represent the reigning monarch at the time the post boxes were installed. Next time you go for a walk, keep your eyes peeled for the red post boxes, and take a look at the initials to decipher who was reigning when it was installed: VR (Queen Victoria) GR (King George V), E II R (Queen Elizabeth II). Have you seen one for our new king?

Address Corner of Brodie Road and Browning Road, Enfield, EN2 0EJ // Getting there Train to Gordon Hill // Hours Accessible 24 hours // Ages 4+

Last Collection Time
Monday to Friday
9.00am

A 4.00pm or later collection is made
from the Postbox at
Lancaster Road Post Office,
Enfield

The latest collection in the area is made
at 7.00pm from
Church Street Post Office,
Church Street Enfield

Saturday
7.00am

03457 740740
www.royalmail.com
0345 6000606
Postbox number: EN2 20

TIP: Take a picnic
and head to the
bandstand at Hilly
Fields Park for
free family-friendly
live music events.

POST·OFFICE

12_ BRUCE CASTLE

Where the king's buddy lived

Bruce Castle Park was Tottenham's first public park. Many mature trees exist here, including the area's oldest oak tree at over 450 years old and therefore classed as ancient. Its hollow trunk is now home to insects and fungi. This tree would have been just a little sprout when King Henry VIII visited Bruce Castle, just a short walk from the tree, when meeting William Compton, the king's most prominent courtier and good friend, who lived here. To discover more trees in the park, head to the front desk inside the castle for a family-friendly Tree Trail.

But before you step inside the beautiful 16th-century building, look over to the left, and you'll see a Tudor tower, the oldest visible part of Bruce Castle. Its original use is a bit murky, with many stories being bandied about, one being its use as a home for keeping hawks ready for hunting.

Bruce Castle, technically a large manor house rather than a castle, remains one of two important Tudor houses in the Greater London area. Once you're inside the main building, the fascinating history begins to unfold. While the main exhibition may be a bit wordy for younger children, there is a vast collection of photos, interesting items (including a sideboard where children can open each door to discover Victorian toys), a great trail around the house, a Tudor dress-up section, and a playroom housing an old photocopier that kids can operate, and an old box camera that they can aim and focus. At the back is a courtyard with seating and giant chess for all to play.

TIP: Love heights? Head to The Dare Skywalk at Tottenham Hotspur Stadium to test your nerves.

Address Lordship Lane,
London, N17 8NU,
+44 (0)208 489 4250,
www.brucecastle.org //
Getting there Tube to
Seven Sisters (Victoria
Line) or Wood Green
(Piccadilly Line) then
bus 123 or 243;
Overground to White
Hart Lane // Hours
Wed–Sun 1–5pm //
Ages 4+

13_CABMEN'S SHELTER

Service through a hatch!

Have you spotted the green wooden huts dotted around London? These are Cabmen's shelters, created in 1875 with the purpose of giving Cabmen a place of shelter where they could grab refreshments at very moderate prices instead of heading to the pub (which was the standard break stop) which led to them consuming too much alcohol.

Inside the huts was seating for around 10 Cabmen, a table and a kitchen area where the attendant would serve up warm grub for the mid shift workers to buy, or they could bring in their own food and the attendant would cook it for them. The Cabmen were forbidden to gamble, drink or swear!

Originally there were 61 of these huts dotted around the streets of London. Thirteen of the Cabmen's shelters still stand, with 12 remaining open and providing refreshments. The 12 open huts serve the same use; continuing to keep London's cabbies fed and watered all year round. Want to take a look inside one of the huts? Well, I'm sorry to say that only licensed black cab drivers are allowed inside the huts. But fret not. We non-cabby folk can order food and drink from the hatch.

If you fancy taking a look and being served via a historical hatch, head to one of these locations: Russell Square WC1 (pictured and café opening times are below), Embankment Place WC2, Grosvenor Gardens SW1, Hanover Square W1, Kensington Park Road W11, Kensington Road W8, Pont Street SW1, St George's Square SW1, Temple Place WC2, Thurloe Place SW7, Warwick Avenue W9 or Wellington Place NW8.

Address 23 Russell Square, London, WC1H 0XG // **Getting there** Tube to Russell Square (Piccadilly Line) // **Hours** Mon–Fri 7am–2pm // **Ages** 0+

TIP: Bloomsbury Lanes offers super fun bowling facilities as well as private karaoke rooms.

14_THE CENTRE OF LONDON

How many miles from home are you?

London may be the capital of England, but do you know where the centre of the capital is? At this spot on the traffic island in Trafalgar Square you'll find a plaque beside a statue of King Charles I marking the 'centre' of London. While this isn't the definitive geometric centre of London, it is from here that all distances as mileage on road signs are measured.

Look at the plaque on the ground and you'll see it reads: 'On the site now occupied by the statue of King Charles I was erected the original Queen Eleanor's cross, a replica of which stands in front of Charing Cross station. Mileages from London are measured from the site of the original cross.'

Where do you live? Can you guess how many miles from home you are?

While you are here, take a look at the statue of Charles I. This is London's oldest bronze statue, commissioned in 1630 by the Lord Treasurer for his house at Roehampton (just over six miles from here). During the Civil War it was ordered to be melted down by Parliament, but instead it was hidden away to evade destruction and was re-erected where you are now by Charles II in 1675. To see some real horses in action, head to Horse Guards Parade on Whitehall, just a stone's throw from here, and watch The Household Cavalry change guard daily at 11am and at 10am on Sundays (subject to larger events). It's a truly unique experience in London not to be missed!

TIP: Victoria Embankment Playground is next to the Savoy Hotel. Here, Claude Monet painted two of his most famous pieces, Waterloo Bridge and Charing Cross Bridge. Both bridges are visible from the playground.

Address Equestrian statue of Charles I, London, WC2N 5DU // Getting there Train or tube to Charing Cross (Northern and Bakerloo Lines) or tube to Embankment (Northern, Bakerloo, District and Circle Lines) // Hours Accessible 24 hours // Ages 0+

15_CHINATOWN

The rudest restaurant in London

Originating in Limehouse (East London) in the 18th century, Chinatown's current location was officially established in the 1960s and now has a cornucopia of restaurants, bars and shops. At its heart, Gerrard Street is book-ended by large vibrant gates and is filled with a canopy of red and gold lanterns that gleam in the sunshine. Chinatown is a wonderful epicentre of oriental wonder. Visit any of the numerous supermarkets for a feel of the shopping aisles in East Asia. As well as browsing fresh produce including fruit, vegetables, meat and fish, you can even see live crabs and lobsters. My stash of noodles bought in SeeWoo got me through my boarding school days when I couldn't face the food we were given.

In Wardour Street you'll find Wong Kei, a restaurant serving up Cantonese flavours, which has a reputation for being the rudest restaurant in London. But don't let that put you off – in fact it's the reason why many people flock here to dine!

I cannot include Chinatown without mentioning Chinese New Year. If you happen to visit at this time of year, you will not be disappointed. Be sure to pick yourself a good spot to see the parade, which usually starts at 10am and ventures through Chinatown before ending in Trafalgar Square where there will be plenty of traditional performances and street vendors.

If you fancy a less crowded venture through Chinatown, grab a treasure map by Treasure Map Trails, which takes you on a journey through Chinatown and Leicester Square and is great fun for families.

TIP: Hidden behind the bustle of Charing Cross Road is Phoenix Garden, a quiet little green space with fish ponds.

Address Gerrard Street, London, W1D 5PT // Getting there Tube to Leicester Square (Piccadilly and Northern Lines) // Hours Accessible 24 hours // Ages 1+

16_ CHURCH STREET CASHPOINT

It's a world first

When did you last use a cash point? With the advance in digital technology to pay for items, and many places becoming card only, the use of cashpoints is dwindling compared with their heyday. Peaking in 2015, there were 70,588 ATMs (Automated Teller Machines) in the UK. This figure has significantly reduced each year since, with the largest reduction of ATMs in London at a 30 per cent plummet by 2023.

There is, however, one ATM in London that won't be going anywhere. Just off Church Street you can shop in the 800-year-old Enfield Market (presumably the produce isn't that old!), have lunch outside The King's Head and watch buskers in the Market House. But before you do any of that, put away your digital device and head to Barclays Bank just on the corner to withdraw some pocket money. It was here in June 1967 that the world's first ATM was installed. Back then, plastic bank cards weren't a thing, and instead customers had paper vouchers encoded with punch holes. This voucher, accompanied by a personal ID number entered into the machine, was used to withdraw £10 notes. Plastic cards were introduced by Barclays in June 1987, making the withdrawal process much easier.

The original cashpoint has been removed and replaced by a blue plaque, but just around the corner you'll find the gold. On the ATM's 50th anniversary in 2017, the hole in the wall was given a golden makeover. Get some cash out (if you can remember your PIN) and treat yourself to a little something in the historic market.

Address 20 The Town, Enfield, EN2 6LS // Getting there Train to Enfield Town // Hours Accessible 24 hours // Ages 4+

BARCLAYS

This gold ATM has been installed to commemorate the 50th anniversary of the world's first cash machine, which was installed by Barclays on this site on 27 June 1967

TIP: Enfield Library offers family events such as Baby Songs and Play, Board Games Club, Toddler Time and Chess Club.

17_CITY DRAGONS

Guarding the boundaries

On any day, from any direction along one of the main thoroughfares, you may decide to venture into the City of London, but beware! For the boundary of the City is guarded by silver dragons each holding a shield decorated with the City of London's coat of arms. Fear not, these aren't real dragons – you can quite easily get past them avoiding a breath of fire to your face. Phew. But why dragons? One theory is that the origin stems from St George, the Patron Saint of England. Legend has it that a vicious dragon was terrorising medieval villagers who, to keep the dragon at bay, would offer him a sheep a day. This resulted in them being short on food, and so it was decided, by order of the king, to sacrifice a child a day instead. Each day a child was selected at random, and on this particular day the king's own daughter was chosen for sacrifice. Luckily for them, George happened to be passing by and was horrified by what was about to happen. He drew his sword and slayed the dragon, setting the villagers free from fear and sacrifice. Each year we celebrate this day on 23 April, in thanks to St George's courage.

You'll also find dragons on two bridges. London boroughs with a connecting bridge share it 50/50, with their boundary mark being the centre of the Thames. This isn't the case with Blackfriars Bridge and London Bridge (pictured), as the south side of the river is within the City of London. So, dragons stand on the south side of these bridges letting entrants know they have crossed the boundary of the City.

Address 5 London Bridge, London SE1 2SX // Getting there Tube or train to London Bridge (Northern or Jubilee Lines) // Hours Accessible 24 hours // Ages 5+

CITY OF
LONDON

TIP: Cross over
London Bridge and climb
to the top of the Monument
to the Great Fire of London,
for views over the City.

18_THE CLIPPER

Hop on, hop off along the river

Uber Boats by Thames Clipper, casually known as 'the Clipper', is by far the best way to travel in London, and it's even covered by your travelcard. While it may not be convenient if you are heading somewhere further inland, if you are headed along the Thames between Putney and Barking, the Clipper is the way to go. I refer to it as the tube on water. With 24 piers being serviced, you can hop on and off wherever you please.

While most people head inside for a nice cosy window seat (which is lovely) I prefer to sit outside at the back of the boat. Here you can feel the wind blowing through your hair as the knots speed up, and from time to time you'll catch a gentle spray of the river's water, which is hilarious for kids. Don't worry – it's not like the River Rafts at Chessington World of Adventures! The back of the boat also doubles up as a fantastic photo op. Time it right so that as you pass under Tower Bridge, you'll have it in the background of your shot. As it's a commuter boat, the freedom and speed at which it travels is a great way to soak up the sights, quickly. On the Clipper, you can get from Embankment to Canary Wharf in 29 minutes.

Throughout the year, the Clipper offers a few surprises. Did you know that in December, Santa likes to ride the Clipper? Check out their socials to see when the big man himself will hop aboard. Many places listed in this book are reachable via the Clipper, so if you wanted to plan a day along the Thames, then you have all you need – transport and tips sorted!

Address Embankment Pier, Victoria Embankment, London, WC2N 6NU, www.thamesclippers.com // Getting there Tube to Embankment (Northern, Circle, District and Bakerloo Lines) // Hours See website for timetable // Ages 0+

TIP: Alight at North Greenwich Pier and take the cable car over the River Thames.

19_COAL DROPS YARD

From coal to curling!

Originating in 1850 to distribute eight million tonnes of coal each year, the area just behind King's Cross station has been transformed over recent years and is wonderfully family friendly. Some of you might be old enough to remember hitting Bagley's nightclub with your mates in the 1990s!

Coal Drops Yard is now in a new era; during the winter months you can see bright winter art installations as well as practise your curling skills at the much-loved Club Curling. In the summer, head to Granary Square for a splash in the water fountain, or sit on the steps overlooking the Regent's Canal to watch a film on the outdoor cinema screen. And Harry Potter fans will love uncovering the magic of Platform 9¾ inside King's Cross railway station. As well as this photo op, you can pop inside the gift shop and grab some Potter merch.

For a bit of tranquillity, head to the canal for a stroll along the towpath. You can download the *Wayward, Wild and Weedy* map to discover the pockets of nature along the way. Hungry? There are bountiful restaurants and cafés to choose from serving up delicious grub, and there's even a quaint library on a barge.

One of the great annual events is the Classic Car Boot Sale where classic cars fill the space, creating a shopper's delight! Bag yourself some pre-loved fashion, head to the Repair Shop to learn how to fix much loved vintage items, join a workshop and throw some shapes to tunes blasting from the DJ booth housed in an old Routemaster bus!

Address Coal Drops Yard, King's Cross, London, N1C 4DQ, www.kingscross.co.uk/coal-drops-yard // **Getting there** Tube or train to King's Cross St Pancras (Northern, Piccadilly, Circle, Victoria, Metropolitan and Hammersmith & City Lines) // **Hours** See website for current information on visiting // **Ages** 0+

TIP: Crumbles Castle Adventure Playground just around the corner is great fun.

20_CROSSBONES GRAVEYARD

A solemn discovery

Festooned with ribbons, flowers and trinkets, the railings running along a seemingly innocuous back street at London Bridge act as the perimeter to a patch of land where a sorrowful discovery occurred.

In the 1990s, construction workers digging tunnels in the area for the Jubilee Line extension, discovered dozens of skulls and bones underground. It was a shock discovery to find remains of paupers from the local area, once known as The Mint (the most violent of slums), buried here prior to 1853.

Left untouched and now in the shadow of the Shard lay approximately 15,000 unnamed paupers and children. Understanding its historical and cultural significance, in 1996 John Crow and Katy Nicholls co-founded the Friends of Crossbones to ensure the sacred land was not lost and forgotten. Over the years this network created a garden here. Years later, working with Bankside Open Spaces Trust, an official public garden of remembrance was opened in memory of those less fortunate. You'll enter this peaceful landscaped space beneath an entrance in the shape of a giant goose wing, spread open to protect visitors as they enter the garden adorned with flowers, plants, shrines and tributes. You'll see a pyramid decorated with oyster shells from neighbouring Borough Market. Now a luxury, oysters were once a poor man's food that many of those resting here would have eaten.

TIP: Conceived of by social reformer Octavia Hill and designed by Elijah Hoole, Red Cross Garden was planned as an 'open air sitting room for the tired inhabitants of Southwark'. The six adjacent red cottages were built to showcase Hill's idea for working-class housing.

At 7pm on the 23rd of each month, people gather for a vigil outside of the gates. Be mindful that this is still a graveyard, and please be respectful.

Address Union Street, London,
SE1 1TA // Getting there Tube to
Borough (Northern Line) // Hours
Wed–Fri noon–2pm // Ages 0+

21_ CROSSNESS PUMPING STATION

What do you think about when you are on the loo?

When sitting on the loo, have you ever thought where the flush takes your waste? The population of London in the 1900s was around six million, and all human waste was dumped into the River Thames, creating a giant festering sewer spreading deadly diseases. Today, you might dream of an apartment overlooking the Thames; back then, there's no way you'd want to be near it. Especially in 1858, the year of the Great Stink! Parliament couldn't bear the stench so rushed through a bill to create a sewage system. In 1865, Crossness Pumping Station opened. And a good job too, as today there's an estimated 10 million people in London, so you can only imagine how grim the Thames would be!

Nicknamed the Cathedral on the Marsh, it may not look so cathedral like from the outside, but the interior is exquisite. You wouldn't guess that originally there were over 1,000 miles of street sewers sending poop downstream to here. The building houses four engines, named after members of the Royal family. On open days you can see one of them pumping away as it would have done all those years ago.

The Engine House is one of the most beautiful examples of Victorian design. Look closely at the columns and try to spot the fruit. Thanks to Victorian humour, the columns are adorned with figs and senna pods – both known laxatives. How's that for a connection with humans to the sewage system? There is also a collection of old toilets that kids love, an education programme featuring crafts and a children's Activity Trail.

TIP: A vintage Routemaster shuttle bus takes visitors from Abbey Wood Station to the RANG Railway, which then takes visitors the last 500 yards from the car park to the site by the Thames.

Address Bazalgette Way, Abbey Wood, London, SE2 9AQ, +44 (0)208 311 3711, www.crossness.org.uk // Getting there Train or tube to Abbey Wood (Elizabeth Line) // Hours Monthly open days and fortnightly tour guiding days (pre-booked) // Ages 5+

22_ CROYDON AIRPORT VISITOR CENTRE

Stand on an aeroplane runway!

In 1928, where would you find the world's largest international airport terminal? You might picture world-famous airports dotted along flight paths across the globe. Croydon Airport was in fact the UK's largest and principal international airport during the interwar period. It was also home to the world's first Air Traffic Control Tower.

Though Croydon Airport closed in 1959, today you can take a guided tour of the Visitor Centre, which includes interactive displays, photographs and historical exhibits on the airport's history. Plus, check out the giant aeroplane at the entrance. Can you find out what type of aircraft this is?

The Visitor Centre is bursting with interesting facts. For example, most of us have heard of the phrase 'Mayday', but do you know where it originated? As the majority of flights in and out of Croydon Airport were between Croydon (obviously!) and Paris, when Senior Radio Officer Stanley Mockford was tasked with creating a pilot distress call, he suggested 'Mayday, Mayday, Mayday' as it was easily interpreted by the French for 'help me': 'M'aidez'.

You'll have a great time exploring Britain's first integrated airport terminal and control tower. Make sure you have your laptop or smartphone ready, as, much like a Taylor Swift concert, tickets for Open Days are released on the first Sunday of every month and book out in the blink of an eye!

Address Airport House, Purley Way, Croydon, CR0 0XZ, +44 (0)752 699 6454, www.historiccroydonairport.org.uk // Getting there Train to Waddon; bus 119 or 289 // Hours First Sun of the month; see website for full information on visiting // Ages 6+

TIP: From Airport House you can take a short walk to the RAF memorial on Purley Way and see a short section of remaining runway extension/taxiway.

23_ CRYSTAL PALACE DINOSAURS

Step into a Jurassic World

Back in the Victorian era, an executive committee was inaugurated to commission a new building in Hyde Park. After 250 design entries that weren't quite right, along came Sir Joseph Paxton, who submitted a design for a Crystal Palace. While not actually made of crystals, the magnificent glass building was constructed. Opened in 1851 by Queen Victoria as the world's first exhibition centre, it attracted over six million visitors. When the exhibition ended, Paxton decided to have the Crystal Palace dismantled and rebuilt in Penge Place, the original name of the area we now know as Crystal Palace, which I think you'll agree sounds far more splendid.

This new location brought much excitement to the area, which became the world's first theme park with a rollercoaster, water jets, entertainment, festivals and even hosted the FA Cup finals. Unfortunately, in 1936 fire damaged the Crystal Palace. It burnt to the ground and was never rebuilt, putting an end to the fun and frivolity at the park. Winston Churchill commented: 'This is the end of an age'.

So how do the dinosaurs fit in? Within the park's landscape is a prehistoric swamp, somewhere Shrek would stay if he were to visit London with Princess Fiona... if they didn't mind sharing with some prehistoric guests. Here you will find the Crystal Palace Dinosaurs. Having undergone a £4-million refurbishment, the dinosaurs are much loved neighbours in the community. If you have ever wondered what a Megalosaurus looks like, then head over to the swamp.

TIP: London Calling is a collection of street art on residential and commercial property. Follow the route on the London Calling Street Art blog to take in all of the artworks.

Address Thicket Road, London, SE20,
+44 (0)203 236 0078, www.cpdinosaurs.org //
Getting there Train to Penge West //
Hours Daily 7.30am–9pm // Ages 3+

24_ DISCOVER CHILDREN'S STORY CENTRE

A magical immersive world

Based in East London for more than 20 years, Discover Children's Story Centre takes children on a wonderful journey. Throughout the centre, families can make up stories, play and learn in live magical Story Worlds and a Story Garden. Story Builders are dedicated to encouraging children to read together and get creative.

Each year brings a new immersive exhibition where visitors can explore the world of great authors including Julia Donaldson, Dr Seuss and Michael Rosen. It's not just the established authors who are showcased here: up-and-coming authors, poets, artists, musicians, illustrators and storytellers visit the centre to run family workshops and events.

With a mission to transform lives through stories, creativity and imagination, Discover Children's Story Centre is a must visit for any child. Ensuring that every child has the chance to visit this fantastic centre, they host a variety of clubs such as Mighty Mega, a free Saturday morning club for disabled children and children with SEN; Story Sandwich, a programme of free visits for adults and children under five who live in temporary housing or are facing homelessness; and After School Stories, a free weekly after-school session for pupils from any school in Newham.

Overall, this centre, run as a charity, has children at its heart, and plays a fantastic role in nurturing their imagination and learning.

> TIP: Head to the top of the ArcelorMittal Orbit observation tower in the Queen Elizabeth Olympic Park, and when you've had enough of the view, exit via the world's longest tunnel slide.

Address 383–387 High Street, London, E15 4QZ, +44 (0)208 536 5555, www.discover.org.uk // Getting there DLR to Stratford High Street or tube to Stratford (Jubilee Line) // Hours Daily 10am–5pm // Ages 0+ to 11 years

25_ DR JOHNSON'S HOUSE

When your bestie is a cat who's as famous as you

On the edge of Gough Square is an impressive house, once the home of Dr Johnson and his best mate Hodge. After being left partially blind and deaf as a baby after an infection, Dr Johnson went on to be a great literary figure in the 18th century, most notably with his book *A Dictionary of the English Language* otherwise known as *Johnson's Dictionary*. Published in 1775, you can get your hands on a first edition for the best part of £60,000. This alone shows its significance. Taking Johnson eight years to complete, it was the first dictionary to explain words by using literary quotations.

Dr Johnson's home on Gough Square is now open to the public and still has many of its original features, including the front door's original anti-burglary devices consisting of a hefty chain with coiled latch and a spiked iron bar. Unlike many houses you can visit, here not much is off limits, as you can enter all the rooms, sit on the chairs and relax on the window seats, looking out and imagining what London was like in Johnson's time. While writing at home, Dr Johnson was accompanied by his cat Hodge, and opposite the house across the square is a statue of Hodge, the world-famous black cat. Johnson spoiled Hodge, who loved oysters. James Boswell wrote in his book *The Life of Samuel Johnson*: 'I never shall forget the indulgence with which he treated Hodge, his cat: for whom he himself used to go out and buy oysters, lest the servants having that trouble should take a dislike to the poor creature...'

TIP: If you like ping pong and pizza, then head to Bounce and grab one of their 17 game tables. Under 18s are allowed in before 6pm Mon−Sat and all day Sunday.

Address 17 Gough Square, London, EC4A 3DE, +44 (0)207 353 3745, www.drjohnsonshouse.org // Getting there Tube to Blackfriars (Circle and District Lines) // Hours Tue–Sat 11am–5pm // Ages 6+

HODGE

26__ELEPHANT SPRINGS

Pack your swimmies and a bucket and spade!

Do you know what the area Elephant & Castle was named after? It's always interesting to learn the origin of place names. They can derive from all sorts of fascinating tales. In this instance, Elephant & Castle was named after a coaching inn. Situated on an old Roman crossroads, travellers would stop at the inn to eat and rest, thus the area took on the inn's name. Though not in its original location due to post-war redevelopment, you can still pop into the Elephant & Castle pub for a bite to eat.

Centuries later, the bustling thoroughfare became known as the 'Piccadilly' of South London, because it was so busy. Over the years, the area has undergone huge regeneration, and continues to transform. Away went the infamous bright pink shopping centre, the first of its kind in Europe, which was demolished in 2021 to make way for a shiny new centre.

Part of the redevelopment was Elephant Springs in Elephant Park. Before you even arrive at the springs, you'll hear the laughter and excitement emanating from children playing freely and splashing about in the water. This fantastic aqua feature comprises cascading water rushing over rocks creating babbling streams. Sandpits, slides, hammocks and water jets elevate the experience as children climb and play on the natural materials used to build the park. This is a spectacular family-friendly community space, which is at the forefront of modern design when it comes to London's redevelopment. Take a packed lunch and spend the day there.

Address 21 Ash Avenue, Elephant Park, London, SE17 1FR, www.elephantpark.co.uk // Getting there Tube to Elephant & Castle (Bakerloo and Northern Lines) or train to Elephant & Castle // Hours Daily 10am–6pm // Ages 1+

TIP: London's first sustainable community market, Mercato Metropolitano, is in an abandoned paper factory. It's now a destination for anyone of any age to enjoy an eclectic selection of authentic food.

27_FAIR PLAY BARNET

Everyone has the right to play

Barnet Council has set the bar high with the opening of this brand new, first-of-its-kind, all abilities playground. Situated in Victoria Recreation Ground, children of all ages and capabilities can come together and play in harmony. The selected apparatus and landscaping have been designed and built to maximise inclusion, offering access play to accommodate wheelchair users. The types of play available include a wheelchair swing, ramped play frame, wheelchair seesaw, a roundabout and a 360-degree swing. You'll also find a musical sensory section, so there are plenty of options for those with additional needs.

The playground opened in 2024, and every element has been well thought out. There is a single entrance/exit so parents and carers have an additional level of assurance that children can't leave without their knowledge, a textured pathway for the visually impaired, a communications board for mixed abilities showing icons of the apparatus available as well as emoticons, a sensory activities panel and a quiet zone. Of course, no playground is complete without classic picnic benches for your packed lunch; however, these benches have been designed so wheelchair users can also sit at the table. The playground also has disabled facilities and parking nearby.

> **TIP:** Football and golf thrust together, creating a super fun mashup of two sports, is available to play at the London Footgolf Centre in Tudor Park.

This groundbreaking project was pioneered by people who are passionate about creating inclusive and accessible spaces for all across the UK. Fair Play Barnet is a revolutionary blueprint, which councils nationwide can (and should) follow.

Address Victoria Recreation
Ground, London, EN4 9BS,
www.barnet.gov.uk // Getting
there Train to New Barnet;
bus 384 to New Barnet Town
Centre then a 10-minute walk //
Hours Accessible 24 hours //
Ages 0+

28_ THE FELLOWSHIP INN

Popcorn and a pint

If you live locally, you might be familiar with this wonderful pub. Steeped in history, The Fellowship Inn was the first pub to be built by a local authority housing estate. On opening in 1924 it was heralded as a new age style of pub. Gone were the days of dingy, crime ridden pubs in old slum districts. All pubs were banished under the anti-alcohol Temperance Movement by the London County Council (LCC) and its new plans to redevelop housing estates. This didn't go down well with locals. But even more outraged were the breweries. Barclay, Perkins & Co. weren't having any of it, so designed a new-wave pub, one that had a dining room to serve food and soft drinks, a roof terrace and recreation hall. They submitted their plans for a licence to build.

It worked! The LCC did away with the no pubs policy, and permission was granted for the pub to be built to serve the community in a more reserved manner. Christmas 1925 saw a local church perform a carol service in the venue, and this was the start of things to come. The pub grew in popularity and would often be full to the brim. In 1926 they built another floor and in 1927 they created a children's room. This blueprint was picked up by other breweries, which followed suit.

Today, the pub is still very much loved by the community. While it has undergone changes to the décor, offerings and management, you can watch live music and sports, play darts, dine and best of all take a seat in The Fellowship Film Club cinema for a free family-friendly screening.

Address Randlesdown Road, London, SE6 3BT, +44 (0)203 876 5883, www.fellowshipinn.co.uk // Getting there Train to Bellingham // Hours Mon–Thu 4–10pm, Fri & Sat noon–11pm, Sun noon–7pm // Ages 0+

TIP: Take on the inflatable assault course at Air Thrill.

29_FITZROVIA MURAL

The more you look, the more you see

On the edge of the hustle and bustle of Tottenham Court Road sits Whitfield Gardens. Recently it has been redesigned and given a much-needed face lift. Gone are the days of rats scurrying underneath the benches and the ground being covered in copious amount of pigeon poop (though pigeons still pop over in the hope of nabbing a fallen sandwich crumb!).

Whitfield Gardens is now a lovely little space to sit and watch the world go by. Hard to miss and set against the whole side of an old building that now houses a friendly newsagent and a fantastic fish and chip shop, you'll see a ground-to-rooftop mural depicting a montage of scenes relevant to the local area.

Sealing the history of Fitzrovia and its residents, the mural, which was commissioned in 1980, is a voice of its time. At the top you'll see building works over a London skyline referencing the planned building projects. Can you spot the vampire-looking man? This is a former leader of the Greater London Council who wasn't so popular with locals. There is a boy clinging to a fence, representing the lack of amenities and green spaces for youngsters, as well as an iconic London red bus and a black cab. The more you look, the more you see. It even includes one of the locals… a pigeon! What else can you see?

The mural has suffered damage over the years, but its recent restoration as part of the Whitfield Gardens facelift has given this historical mural a new lease of life for many years to come.

TIP: Do you think you can play Monopoly without having a family row? Give it a go at the super Monopoly Lifesized game on Tottenham Court Road.

Address 8 Tottenham Street, London, W1T 4RB // Getting there Tube to Goodge Street (Northern Line) // Hours Accessible 24 hours // Ages 3+

30_ FORTNUM AND MASON CLOCK

What to do with a candle stump?

Fortnum and Mason is a quintessentially British department store that has hardly changed since it opened. Its window displays alone are a feast for the eyes, especially at Christmas, and attract thousands of admirers.

The shop was founded by two pals, William Fortnum and Hugh Mason. Fortnum was a footman to Queen Anne, and one of his tasks in this role was to ensure that the palace candles were replaced daily – this was in a time long before we had lightbulbs! At the end of his shift, he was allowed to keep any old candle stumps. What for, you might ask? Well, he sold them on and had a very successful candle-stump business.

So how does Mason fit in? When Fortnum retired as a footman, and after gaining years of insight into palace life, he suggested to his landlord Mason that they open up a shop together with the purpose of supplying goods to the palace and local aristocrats. The pair were so successful that the business quickly grew and became famous for supplying exotic produce not seen in England before.

Nowadays, the opulent store still retains its quality and has an array of unique items for sale. It also offers family events throughout the year, such as Children's Afternoon Tea and Storytelling with Father Christmas. At the front of the store, look up and you will notice a delightful clock. On the hour, every hour, out pop figures of Mr Fortnum and Mr Mason. They make their way outside and face each other before returning inside for the next hour, presumably to serve customers…

Address 181 Piccadilly, St James', London, W1A 1ER, +44 (0)207 734 8040, www.fortnumandmason.com // Getting there Tube to Piccadilly Circus (Bakerloo and Piccadilly Lines) // Hours Clock accessible 24 hours; shop Mon–Sat 10am–8pm, Sun noon–6pm // Ages 2+

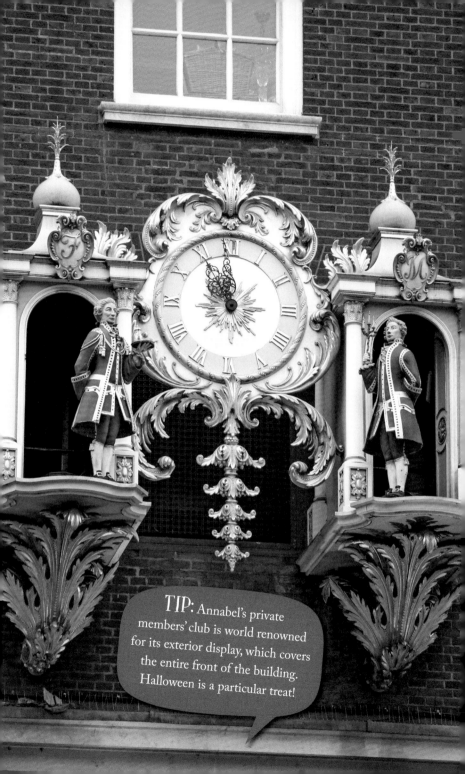

TIP: Annabel's private members' club is world renowned for its exterior display, which covers the entire front of the building. Halloween is a particular treat!

31_FOUNDLING TOKENS

Trinkets to identify children

Hidden trinkets dotted around Marchmont Street symbolise much more than a fun treasure hunt. Sporadically placed along the pavement, you'd be forgiven for not noticing them as you walk along this quiet Bloomsbury street.

Just around the corner is the Foundling Museum. Constructed on the site of the Foundling Hospital, the museum tells the story of the UK's first children's charity designed to care for London's most vulnerable children. Established in 1739, the hospital was set up by Thomas Coram.

Poverty-stricken parents could leave their young child at the Foundling Hospital to be cared for away from the harsh reality of living an impoverished life. For 200 years the Foundling Hospital looked after a staggering 25,000 children, keeping them safe and well cared for. But admittance wasn't easy, as places were in high demand. In fact, it was a lottery with coloured balls indicating whether your child would be accepted. Parents, usually mothers, would pick a ball out of a bag and the colour depicted their admittance: black – refusal, white – tentative acceptance based on a health check, red – they joined a queue awaiting a space if a 'white ball' candidate was rejected due to ill health.

Mothers whose child was accepted would leave a token as an identification for collecting their child, should their circumstances change. This permanent installation represents trinkets given by destitute mothers handing over their precious children to the Foundling Hospital in the hope of seeing them again one day.

TIP: Coram Fields (named after Thomas Coram) is a child-only zone! No adults are permitted unless accompanied by a child. There is a fantastic playground, café and regular child-friendly events.

Address Marchmont Street, London, WC1N 1NJ // Getting there Tube to Russell Square (Piccadilly Line) // Hours Accessible 24 hours // Ages 5+

32_ GABRIEL'S WHARF

Head to the beach!

Bring your bucket and spade, because at low tide you can play on the sandy beach of the River Thames. You can even dip your toes in the water if you are brave enough! On some days you'll see sand sculptors creating magnificent objects like dragons or giant people on the shore while the tide is out. Access to the beach is via a gate along the railings of the riverside and down some metal steps.

After some fun on the beach, head back up the steps and into Gabriel's Wharf for a spot of small business shopping and a bite to eat from one of the many superb food spots, plus take a look at the huge mural adorning the old brick wall adjacent to the now closed London Studios where many live TV shows were broadcast from. Can you spot any people in the mural windows?

You might be wondering 'Who is Gabriel?'. Well, the name started with Christopher Gabriel, a maker of woodworking planes that are used to skim wood leaving a smooth, flat surface. In around 1812, his sons decided to enter the timber business, and began importing and exporting from the wharf. Fast forward to 1919, the company closed the wharf, but the name stayed and the wharf has since reopened and grown to become a hugely popular destination for those roaming along the South Bank.

Just next to the wharf is a small park where you can picnic on the grass, or sit on a bench looking across the river. Throughout the year the wharf hosts many events, including a diverse line-up of live music, DJs and entertainment for all to enjoy.

TIP: Wander along the Thames Path to the OXO Tower, where you can get the lift up to the viewing platform and see unbroken views of St Paul's and the city's skyline.

Address Upper Ground, London,
SE1 9PP, +44 (0)207 021 1650,
www.coinstreet.org/gabriels-wharf //
Getting there Train or tube to Waterloo
(Northern, Jubilee, Waterloo and City,
and Bakerloo Lines) // Hours Accessible
24 hours // Ages 0+

33__THE GARDEN MUSEUM

A view from a medieval tower

The Garden Museum is the next-door neighbour of Lambeth Palace, home to the Archbishop of Canterbury, who officiated the ceremony of King Charles III's Coronation in Westminster Abbey in 2023. He also has the most beautiful pad… Imagine living in a palace on the River Thames!

Having such a wonderful riverside location, it's easy to see why the Garden Museum is also situated here, right inside the deconsecrated church of St Mary-at-Lambeth. Also on this site rests the preserved tomb of the Tradescant family. John Tradescant was an early gardener and plant hunter who travelled the world collecting plants in the 17th century. The Garden Museum tells more on this fascinating character and much besides.

Learning about how and why we garden, you can explore the permanent collection of artefacts and tools from gardening throughout history and marvel at botanical photography and art. There is also a tranquil courtyard garden known as an Eden of rare plants. The museum also offers family activities exploring the theme of gardens and nature through art, craft, cooking and plant science, as well as SEN sessions.

The gem of the Garden Museum is the medieval tower. Make your way up 131 steps for a glorious view across the Thames to the Houses of Parliament and have a nose into the Lambeth Palace gardens down below. While not open to the public often, check out Lambeth Palace open days (separate from the Garden Museum) to take a wander around the exclusive gardens. Dogs are welcome on open days too.

Address 5 Lambeth Palace Road, London, SE1 7LB, +44 (0)207 401 8865, www.gardenmuseum.org.uk // Getting there Tube to Lambeth North (Bakerloo Line) // Hours Daily 10am–5pm // Ages 0+

TIP: Archbishop's Park and playground is just around the corner and is fun for kids of all ages.

34_GERMAN LAMPPOST

A gift from a twin

Have you ever heard of town twinning? Many places around the world twin with another friendly nation and may send a gift to commemorate this kinship. Right here in Hammersmith is an example of this. As you amble along the north side of the Thames Path towards Hammersmith Bridge, past boat houses and a quaint little park called Furnivall Gardens, you'll arrive at a beautiful large riverside house whose side wall faces the gardens. Depending on the time of year you visit, the wall may be covered in vibrant purple wisteria. Among the floral décor you'll see a lamp set on the wall, below which is a plaque that reads: 'The lamp above this plaque was formerly used to light a street in West Berlin. It was presented by Herr Willi Brandt, the Mayor of West Berlin to Councillor Stanley Atkins, J. P., the Worshipful the Mayor of Hammersmith, as a token of friendship between the two communities on the occasion of the Jumelage held in this Borough, 1st June 1963.'

TIP: Just beyond Hammersmith Bridge is Riverside Studios – a theatre, cinema, TV studio, art and events hub offering lots for the whole family. Plus, there's a riverside restaurant.

Town twinning (or sister cities if outside of Europe) was introduced to build links and understanding between different cultures and local communities, and many exchange students visit their twin city to study. The idea grew in popularity after World War II and almost every London borough has a twin or two. Some examples are Haringey with Larnaca in Cyprus, Greenwich with Tema in Ghana, Lewisham with Matagalpa in Nicaragua, and Waltham Forest with Mirpur in Pakistan. Do you know if your home town has a twin?

Address 22 Lower Mall, London, W6 9DJ // Getting there Tube to Hammersmith (District, Piccadilly and Hammersmith & City Lines) // Hours Accessible 24 hours // Ages 0+

35_ GO APE

Exploring London's treetops

Battersea Park may not be the first place you think of for monkey business, but it's here you can experience what it's like to be one of our primitive friends overlooking the cityscape from within the tree tops. For over 20 years, Go Ape has innovated fun and exploration at great heights. Simply arrive, harness up, clip on, and GO! Commence the Treetop Adventure where you'll encounter unsteady bridges and tricky crossings in order to master loops, before zipping through the tree canopy back to ground. Want more? Experience dizzying heights as you embark on the Treetop Challenge, an exhilarating high rope obstacle course with awesome views over Battersea Park and the London skyline. In a rush? No problem. Take on the Treetop Challenge Express – just as much fun but half the time.

Once back on solid ground you'll be pleased to see the café, where you can enjoy refreshments while your heart rate returns to normal. There's also a toilet should the excitement have got a little too much for you. Before leaving, head to the shop to pick up a memento to celebrate your achievement. Thirsty for more? Go Ape is an excellent choice for children's birthday parties, and you can even add party bags to the order, so that's another job off your list! Be sure to check details on the website for all activities, as they are broken into height and age bands.

Overall, Go Ape is a great physical and mental activity that kids (and adults) very much enjoy. Though you'll find me firmly on the ground, watching with a cup of tea.

Address Battersea Park, London, SW11 4NJ, +44 (0)160 389 5500, www.goape.co.uk // Getting there Train or tube to Battersea Park (Northern Line) // Hours Thu–Tue 10.30am–5pm, Wed 11.30am–5pm // Ages 4+

TIP: Get close to a Brazilian black tarantula at Battersea Park Children's Zoo.

36_GOBOAT PADDINGTON

Self-drive through the London canals

Have you ever fancied being the captain of your own boat? Good news – thanks to GoBoat, you can. The electric-powered boat offers a smooth easy-to-run option for exploring London's waterways. GoBoat has a few bases dotted around, including Paddington, Canary Wharf, Kingston and Thames Ditton.

In this chapter we will explore GoBoat Paddington, where you can discover the Regent's Canal up close, so close in fact that you feel like a duck plodding along on the water. A two-hour round trip is the perfect way to explore the canal and soak up the atmosphere from Paddington through to Little Venice all the way to Camden and back.

London can seem very fast paced, but once aboard one of these little boats you have no choice but to sit back, relax and watch the world go by as you sail past real houseboats, boat restaurants including a cheese barge and The BoAt Pod, a 1970s-inspired recording studio and radio station built on a boat! You'll even sail through the 272-yard Maida Hill Tunnel. The boats have a speed cap, so if you are scared of the dark, you might want to close your eyes and think happy thoughts until you exit the other end!

Each boat seats eight people and you are welcome to take a picnic on board. Children are, of course, welcome, so it makes for a great family trip. Life jackets are provided for kids. There is a choice of trip duration: one, two or three hours. If you are doing one of the longer routes, just make sure you nip to the loo before you set sail!

Address Merchant Square, London, W2 1AS, +44 (0)203 887 6955, www.goboat.co.uk // Getting there Tube or train to Paddington (Elizabeth, Circle, District and Bakerloo Lines) // Hours Mon–Thu 10am–8.30pm, Fri 9am–8.30pm, Sat & Sun 9.30am–8.30pm // Ages 0+

TIP: Can you find the Paddington Bear statue in Paddington Station?

37_GOD'S OWN JUNKYARD

The Kings of Neon

Neon lights adorn every inch of this warehouse. It's a truly mesmerising space to immerse yourself in, and of course shop if you feel your home is missing that show-stopping piece. From new and old neon signs to film props and fairground lights, it seems like every Pantone colour is ticked off! But this isn't the first time you'll have seen a God's Own Junkyard neon sign: you've probably walked past a great many, as most of Central London's neon signs that you see outside businesses were created here.

It all started with Dick Bracey, who worked on fun fairs, carnivals and circuses, and began collecting and storing items he picked up along the way, most notably the colourful signs. Later, his son Chris started creating neon art. One day, Paul Raymond of the Raymond Revuebar and the Windmill Club in Soho approached Chris to create signs for his businesses. Now, approximately 80 per cent of Soho's neon signs were created at God's Own Junkyard. The mesmerising bespoke lights are all handmade on site, from sketch to glass burning, gas and installation. Neon enthusiasts travel from near and far to enter this vibrant wonderland, as do celebrities such as Kate Moss, Lady Gaga and Elton John.

Marcus, neon light artist and Chris' son, started working with his dad and putting signs up from the age of eight years old. This is a great example of a successful family-run London business that continues to light up London's streets. Now with children of his own, let's hope the business continues for years to come.

Address Unit 12, Ravenswood Industrial Estate, Shernhall Street, London, E17 9HQ, +44 (0)208 521 8066, www.godsownjunkyard.co.uk // **Getting there** Tube to Walthamstow Central (Victoria Line) and a 15-minute walk; Overground to Wood Street // **Hours** Fri & Sat 11am–10pm, Sun 11am–6pm // **Ages** 6+

TIP: Hire a rowing boat at Hollow Ponds and bob along to the sounds of nature.

38__THE GOLDEN HINDE

A hidden ship

Travelling via boat along the Thames between Southwark Bridge and London Bridge, you might notice a large ship docked in the shadows in between buildings. It's an intriguing sight. To access the ship via land, you must head through the old cobbled streets of London Bridge past Southwark Cathedral towards the river.

There you will find the Golden Hinde, a permanently docked full-size replica of the Golden Hind galleon that was the first English ship ever to circumnavigate the globe, in 1577. The ship was later captained by Sir Francis Drake, of Spanish Armada fame, who also happened to be Queen Elizabeth I's favourite privateer (just an official sort of pirate really). The reconstruction, which took two years to achieve, was built at Hinks & Son shipyard in Apple-dore. All very interesting, but are you allowed onto the ship? YES! Head onboard to discover the fascinating history of what it was like to live and sail aboard a 16th-century ship, through one of the official tours. Alternatively, you can enter with general admission and grab an audio guide.

Staff dress as old crew mates and can certainly hold a crowd. As well as family events throughout the year, you can also have children's birthday parties on board, which are hosted by the super energetic crew. Why not try your hand at an escape-room game, or go to a talk on terrifying female pirates like Ching Shih? You can take your pi-rate pooch too, as the ship is dog friendly. All children should expe-rience life onboard the Golden Hinde!

Address St Mary Overie's Dock, Cathedral Street, London, SE1 9DE, +44 (0)207 403 0123, www.goldenhinde.co.uk // Getting there Tube or train to London Bridge (Northern or Jubilee Lines) // Hours Daily Nov–Mar 10am–5pm, Apr–Oct 10am–6pm // Ages 5+

TIP: Venture along the narrow lane and onto Bankside, where you will find Shakespeare's Globe.

39_ GREENWICH FOOT TUNNEL

A claustrophobic's nightmare

There are many ways to get to Greenwich, depending on where you are travelling from. One of our favourite ways is aboard the Thames Clipper (like the tube, but on a boat). When you alight at the pier, you'll be amazed at the glorious sight of the Cutty Sark, a stunning vessel. You can step aboard and see what it was like to be a sailor 150 years ago. But this chapter is more about what you can do under the water, rather than on top.

To the right of the pier, as you step back on land, is a large seating area with a wonderful view of Canary Wharf. You'll also see the domed entrance to the Greenwich foot tunnel which, via a lift, takes you around 50 feet deep under the Thames. The tunnel leads to the north side of the river where you emerge at Island Gardens. Here you can look back across the river to see the Old Royal Naval College in all its glory. It's very nice over there, but, if you have an over-active imagination and can only focus on the old walls of the tunnel caving in and waves of water flooding in, it makes for a rather claustrophobic and hasty walk to the other side! However, you've got to do it at least once, right?

TIP: Island Gardens, if you are brave enough to cross through the tunnel, is a quaint little park, perfect for getting your heart rate back to normal.

Designed by civil engineer Sir Alexander Binnie, who also designed the Blackwall Tunnel and Vauxhall Bridge, the Greenwich Foot Tunnel was completed and opened in 1902. To this day, thousands of pedestrians venture through this foot tunnel each month. If you notice a lot of water present in the tunnel, it undergoes regular 'wet cleaning', so don't worry, it's not a leak!

Address Greenwich Foot Tunnel,
London, SE10 9HT // Getting
there DLR to Cutty Sark // Hours
Accessible 24 hours // Ages 0+

40_ HAMPSTEAD HILL GARDEN

An Edwardian sanctuary

The perfect setting for a romance film, Hampstead Hill Garden and Pergola is one of the most splendid Edwardian spots in London. Entering feels as though you have stumbled across a lost world. Climbing floral vines envelop rows of columns that look simply dreamy. Set in the vastness of Hampstead Heath, the hill garden overlooks the West Heath. Envisaged by Lord Leverhulme, who in 1904 bought Inverforth House – then known as The Hill – and later purchased more of the surrounding land, he pictured a pergola as a magnificent setting for garden parties and summertime strolls.

Landscape architect Thomas Mawson was the creative mastermind behind the design you see today. This is in fact one of the best surviving examples of his work and has been admired by thousands of people over the years. In 1905 his design began its journey to fruition. Coincidently, the Northern Line extension was being built simultaneously. Needing somewhere to dump all of the soil extracted to make the tunnel, the contractors arranged a deal with Lord Leverhulme who agreed (for a fee, of course) to have the soil dumped on his land, soil that was needed to help build his and Thomas' garden development.

TIP: Pack your swimwear and head to Hampstead Mixed Pond for a spot of splashing in the natural bathing pond.

Nowadays you can stroll through the pergola, look over at the views of the heath, wander by the pond, take in the beauty of the surrounding flowers or simply sit and admire the charming structure. Many people head to the pergola for personal photo shoots celebrating life moments. Once you are there, it's easy to see why.

Address The Pergola, Inverforth Close, London, NW3 7EX, www.cityoflondon.gov.uk // Getting there Tube to Hampstead (Northern Line) // Hours Daily 8.30am – 7.30pm; check seasonal hours // Ages 0+

41_HEADSTONE MANOR

The people and the place

How much do you know about Harrow? Until discovering Headstone Manor and Museum, I knew very little. This inspiring Grade I-listed building makes for a fascinating discovery of the people and history within Harrow. Travelling back in time as you wander from room to room you will be enlightened with facts and tales before ending up in the early medieval house. Much has changed over the centuries, and architecture fans can see the journey of restoration, as well as the discoveries uncovered during the builds. Children will love investigating the moat, watching ducks dipping by.

Specifically for families, Headstone has countless offerings. Throughout the year you can enter the Bakehouse playroom and dress up as a Tudor cook, follow the Bill the Duck trail, explore the nature trail, and give the kids the 'Play Prompt Cards' to use across the estate. Annual trails such as Gnomes for Easter, Pumpkins for October, and Eliza's pet trail for summer are brilliant ways to discover the grounds together. There is also a yearly Teddy Bears' Picnic where children bring along their favourite bear for a fun day of singing and crafts. The Mini Museum series is set in the Great Hall. Join Bill the Duck for stories and adventures about life in Harrow. Play backpacks and sensory backpacks are available in the house, as are treasure hunts – always popular with kids.

Whether you live in Harrow or are planning your first trip, make sure you pop over to Headstone Manor and Museum. Bill will be waiting to greet you!

TIP: Get snapping at the Kodak Monument, immortalising where the Kodak factory stood until 2016, when digital images grew in demand, so there was less need for film.

Address Headstone Recreation
Ground, Pinner View, Harrow,
HA2 6PX, +44 (0)208 863 6720,
www.headstonemanor.org //
Getting there Train, Overground
or tube to Harrow and Wealdstone
(Bakerloo Line) // Hours
Tue–Sun 10am–4pm // Ages 0+

HARROW'S HEYD.
OF GEORGIAN GLAMOUR

During the Georgian period (1714 – 1837) it was very important
for anyone with aspirations of rank to establish their place
in society. Winning approval from the 'right' people was a
stepping stone to even greater wealth and status. Fashion
was everything, and that meant fashionable architecture,
entertainment and landscaping as well as clothes.

42_HUNTERIAN MUSEUM

Your leg bone's connected to your knee bone...

Have you ever been intrigued as to what the inside of your body looks like? The Hunterian Museum holds England's largest public display of human and animal physiology and anatomy. You'll be fascinated by the amazing collection of specimens, sculptures and paintings that tell the often grisly story of surgery through time.

The collection was begun by army surgeon anatomist John Hunter. When he wasn't treating patients, he spent most of his time building up a vast assortment of human and animal specimens from all over the world – around 14,000 at his death. Some of his collecting methods were what you might call decidedly dodgy though.

Exploring the human make up using real specimens has permitted the development of medical knowledge. While some of the human remains may be unsettling to view, we must respect that each person whose body has been studied has helped medicine and surgery get to where it is today, helping millions of people worldwide. You'll see examples of early prosthetics, including a silver nose painted to the skin tone of the wearer, which is affixed to glasses frames to sit the nose in place.

As well as humans, you can take a closer look at animals, amphibians and insects. Did you know that the female Surinam toad incubates her fertilised eggs on her back? When ready to enter the world, they disembark as young adults. And I bet you were thinking they just laid eggs! The museum also hosts family events with no age restriction; you decide if the content is suitable for your child.

Address 43 Lincoln's Inn Fields, London, WC2A 3PE, +44 (0)207 405 3474, www.hunterianmuseum.org // Getting there Tube to Chancery Lane (Central Line) // Hours Tue–Sat 10am–5pm // Ages 0+

TIP: A short walk will get you to Forbidden Planet, a sanctuary for any comic book fan.

43_IMPERIAL PARK

Planes, trains and a football squad

Part of the wider Imperial Wharf, on its completion in 2009 Imperial Park was the newest riverside park to be established for 50 years. A new overground station was also opened, making Imperial Wharf an ideal spot for commuters, especially as the estate incorporated brand new luxury apartments, town houses and affordable housing. In line with the hundreds of residents moving in, new shops, cafés and restaurants were also built. And let's not forget the kids. Naturally, the park houses a playground for those little legs among us.

There are two main entrances to this beautifully landscaped park. One is off Townmead Road and the other is via the Thames Path; both are connected by a tree-lined avenue with a water fountain at the centre. Within the park are also three sensory gardens that focus on aroma, sight and touch. Sitting on a bench facing across the river you may see helicopters coming in to land at the helipad opposite. You'll also see the bridge where you can watch the trains coming in and out of Imperial Wharf Station. If that wasn't enough transport, planes fly overhead towards Heathrow. For any Chelsea football fans out there, if you time your visit right, you'll see the men's football squad going for a walk together. I saw this once back in the Eden Hazard days.

TIP: Ever fancied yourself as Spiderman? Clip 'n' Climb is a great place to practise your wall climbing skills.

If you fancy a bite to eat, head to The Waterside, which has two river terraces, or for a more traditional British pub venture past the old terraced houses to The Fulham Arms. Both options have a children's menu.

Address Townmead Road, London, SW6 2PT, +44 (0)207 926 9000 //
Getting there Overground or tube to Imperial Wharf (West London Line) //
Hours Daily 7am–8pm // Ages 0+

44_JOSEPH GRIMALDI PARK

Clowning about on a coffin

Coulrophobia (cool-ruh-foe-bee-uh) is a fear of clowns, suffered by many adults and children, so if you are one of them, continue reading with caution!

One of the world's most famous clowns, Joseph Grimaldi, has a park named after him, and it is here that he was laid to rest in 1837. Keeping in the spirit of clowning around, you are invited to dance on Grimaldi's grave. Well, not his actual grave as that would be very rude! In 2010 artist Henry Krokatsis created a permanent interactive installation encapsulating the spirit of Grimaldi's innovative entertaining style.

Heralded as inventing the modern-day clown, Grimaldi was born in a London slum in 1778 and made his stage debut at the age of three years old. He would go on to become the most popular English entertainer of the time. Once a leading player in the harlequinade (a theatrical comedy) his role of the clown became affectionately known as 'Joey'. This friendly nickname is still used to describe clowns today.

In the Joseph Grimaldi Park, not only can you play on the swings, you'll also find two coffin shapes lying side by side. Though they aren't just to be looked at, you are encouraged to dance on them. Why? They create musical notes with every step! It is suggested that you dance a musical rendition of the song Grimaldi made famous called *Hot Codlins*, which tells a tale of baked apples sold in the old street markets. However, this song isn't widely known nowadays so go wild and hop, skip and clown around to your own musical tune!

> **TIP:** Known locally as the 'Heart of Angel', Chapel Market is where you'll find an array of food, toys and gadgets on sale from the friendly market traders. Might you find a Hot Codlin? Perhaps.

Address 11 Collier Street, London, N1 9JU,
+44 (0)207 527 2000 // Getting there Tube
to Angel (Northern Line) or train or tube to King's
Cross St Pancras (Northern, Piccadilly, Circle,
Hammersmith & City, Victoria and Metropolitan
Lines) // Hours Daily 8am – dusk // Ages 0+

45_THE KENTISH DROVERS

Keeping the cattle fat!

The Old Kent Road is one of the oldest roads in the country. Paved by the Romans, it has been the primary route between London and the Kent coast for centuries. At the turning onto Commercial Way, you'll see an unassuming building on the corner, which has housed many different businesses over time. Originating as a pub called Kentish Drovers Tavern, it is now a Grade II-listed building.

Look up and you'll see an intricate hand-painted mural depicting the drovers' journey. Historically drovers (people who move cattle from one place to another) would move their livestock from Kent to Smithfield Market along this route. The Kentish Drovers pub was built in 1840 and frequented by these men who needed a respite.

As the journey from Kent would take so long, they would let their cattle graze here, sometimes for weeks, in order to fatten them up, which would increase their sale value when arriving at Smithfield Market. If you look closely at the mural (or as close as you can from street level) you'll see men resting at the old tavern, others guiding horses, cattle, a young boy running, geese, a couple of ladies having a chat and an older lady who appears to have dropped some potatoes (or buns?). Can you see the windmill in the distance?

The mural has succumbed to damage over the years, but now a restoration project by Southwark Council and The Heritage of London Trust will return the mural to its original glory and it will be used to teach local school children about the history of Old Kent Road.

TIP: The Prince of Peckham is a home from home. With its youthful and vibrant selection of events, children can enjoy free sessions such as storytelling. Plus, they have a great kids' menu!

Address 720 Old Kent Road, London, SE15 1NG // Getting there Overground to Queen's Road Peckham // Hours Accessible 24 hours // Ages 4+

46_KIDSPACE ROMFORD

Arrive and go!

The ultimate palace, jam packed with adrenaline and excitement, awaits all children who pass through Kidspace Romford's doors. Let's begin with my favourite space, the Oceanarium. Dive deep to the bottom of the ocean without having to hold your breath, as this immersive experience takes you up close to sea creatures of the deep. The first of its kind in Europe, this Oceanarium is mesmerising for young minds. They can touch computer-generated fish, which flinch and swim away. Every part of the space is covered, so you truly feel like you are standing on the sea bed.

That's the peaceful part out of the way, so let the mayhem commence! The Thunderdome causes jovial riots among buddies as they fire soft balls at each other across the tiered arena. Kids could get lost for hours exploring the huge play frame that incorporates layer upon layer of tunnels, climbing zones and tube slides. If kids want to zoom around the circuit, they can jump in the driving seat and whizz around the indoor Go Kart track. Keen for more? Kids can harness up and ascend the climbing wall to finesse their climbing skills ready for the great outdoors, one day! Why not see who can reach the top of the wall in the shortest time? Back down on the ground, under fours take over the Toddler Zone, and during term time Learn and Play sessions offer dancing, arts and crafts, and sensory play.

Once the fun is over, head to the dining area which offers a huge variety of food, so even fussy eaters will be fed.

> TIP: One kid's junk is another kid's treasure! Head to Bonzer car boot sale for a bargain.

Address The Brewery, Waterloo Road, Romford, RM1 1AU, +44 (0)170 859 8930, www.kidspaceadventures.com // Getting there Train, Overground or tube to Romford (Elizabeth Line) // Hours Mon–Thu 10am–7pm, Fri–Sun 9am–7.30pm // Ages 0+

47_KYOTO GARDEN

A gift from a friend

Holland Park is huge! In fact, it's the Royal Borough of Kensington and Chelsea's largest park, and because of its size, it has so much to offer. The adventure playground for ages 5–14 years has all the bells and whistles required of such a space: slides, zip wires, various climbing apparatus and accessible equipment. It also has activities to encourage youngsters to get up close with the natural world around them; habitat panels and rubbing plaques are just a couple of interactive items that help broaden their knowledge, and just across the way is the toddlers' playground.

The wider park has further offerings. Opera Holland Park, surrounded by gardens and woodland, offers a three-month summer opera festival, including family-friendly performances such as Sergei Prokofiev's *Peter and the Wolf*, which is 30 minutes long and suitable for ages 0+. Unsure if opera is for you? There are free lunchtime recitals on the steps of the building, so pitch up on the grass and see what you think.

One of the most beautiful gardens in Holland Park is the Kyoto Garden. Constructed as part of The Japanese Festival in 1991 and built by the Kyoto Chamber of Commerce, it was given to this London borough as a token of friendship between Great Britain and Japan.

TIP: Japan House, the cultural home of Japan in London, has lots to see and discover, including family sessions.

The garden is a delightfully tranquil pocket within the larger park. While it is popular with visitors, it is by no means noisy. The garden is a perfect spot for quiet reflection and relaxation, set to the soundscape of the flowing waterfall.

Address Holland Park, Holland Park Avenue, London, W11 4UA // Getting there Tube to Holland Park (Central Line) // Hours Daily 7.30am–8pm // Ages 0+

48_LEAKE STREET ARCHES

Look what Banksy started

Hidden below Waterloo Station are Leake Street Arches, otherwise known as the graffiti tunnel, for obvious reasons! Here, artists are legally allowed to leave their mark on London's largest graffiti wall. Starting in 2008, the artist Banksy and a group of his artistic buddies headed to Leake Street armed with spray cans aplenty to let loose on the arches as part of The Cans Festival. No visit is ever the same, as there are always new works popping up.

You can even have a go yourself and leave your stamp on one of London's famous art spots. Taking part in a graffiti workshop (for those aged 12 years and over), you'll suit up in white overalls, a mask and gloves, and be guided on the art of graffiti. Using a simple guide on how to use a spray can, you can go along to the workshop with an idea already in mind, or think of a creation on the spot, letting your creativity take over!

Take a look at all of the art that has accumulated over time. The more you look, the more you see! Which do you prefer? The vibrant colourful works? Or the monochrome black and white style? The fierce bird or perhaps the giant baby? If you visit twice, you're not likely to see all the same art again; it's an ever-changing canvas of the mind.

Leake Street Arches provides a multi-function space offering a dive bar showing American sports and a Polish restaurant serving up traditional national dishes. Plus, as well as events throughout the year they also have Draughts, a super-cool board game café where you can even bring your dog!

Address Leake Street, London, SE1 7NN, www.leakestreetarches.london // Getting there Train or tube to Waterloo (Northern, Jubilee, Waterloo and City and Bakerloo Lines) // Hours Accessible 24 hours // Ages 10+

TIP: Jubilee Playground is in the shadow of the London Eye, which makes for a great photo op while having fun.

49_LEINSTER GARDENS

It's a fake!

London is an architectural dream! At every turn you'll stumble across façades from different times. Whether it's Baroque or Victorian, Regency or Edwardian, Georgian or Modern, around each corner you'll find individuality and history.

As you look at images of residential streets in London, try and guess which part of London it is. There is a certain distinctiveness between the areas. A residential street in Muswell Hill is different from a residential street in Hackney; the same goes for Notting Hill versus Dulwich. Each area has a distinct style of living that has evolved over time.

Venturing along a seemingly normal Victorian terraced street in Bayswater, you might want to stop and take a closer look at numbers 23 and 24. Behind the windows and doors is… nothing! This is indeed a fake house, with nothing but a façade to create the illusion of an unbroken row of terraced houses. If you loop round to the other side of the house onto Porchester Terrace, you'll see why.

Once on Porchester Terrace, and if you are tall enough, you'll see down to the rail tracks of the world's first underground railway, the Metropolitan Railway. The route was built with the 'cut and cover' method, which meant digging into the ground to build the tunnel and then covering it up again. However, Leinster Gardens was left open aired. Back then, we didn't have the slick underground trains we have today – earlier underground trains ran on coal and steam, so the tunnels needed vents to release the build-up of emissions.

TIP: The Peter Pan statue in Hyde Park was unveiled overnight by the book's author J.M. Barrie. He wanted children to stumble across the statue the next day as if it had appeared by magic.

106

Address 24 Leinster Gardens,
London, W2 3AN // Getting
there Tube to Bayswater (Circle
and District Lines) // Hours
Accessible 24 hours // Ages 0+

LEINSTER
GARDENS W2
CITY OF WESTMINSTER

50_LEWIS OF LONDON

An udder delight

How does ice cream grow? My daughter asked this as we were on our way to the ice cream farm. Not a ridiculous question, since we have previously been to strawberry and pumpkin farms to pick our own, so I can see why this question was born. Thankfully, there is a display board right by the entrance that tells the story of the farm, including how ice cream became a part of it.

The farm has been in the same family since 1968. Growing a dairy herd, they initially began producing milk, and in 2014 ice cream was introduced. As the cows are based at the farm, there are zero milk miles; it literally comes from the field to the customer, with a bit of creativity and flavour added along the way. We opted for a Dinosaur Blue, which I expected to taste like berries, but it had a burst of banana flavour – truly delicious and full of natural ingredients.

As well as the ice cream parlour serving up over 30 flavours, children will love the activities. Enter Moo-land to ride-on mini tractors, bounce on bouncy cows, and play with diggers on the sandy 'beach' while adults relax in deck chairs. A favourite with kids is the mini ice cream parlour where they can grab an apron and play at making ice cream and serving customers. There's also an inflatable fun zone during the summer. This would also make an ideal spot for a kids' birthday party; they have great packages available in the party cabins or teepee. While the farm is on the very outskirts of Barnet, it's worth a trip for the sheer aMOOsement!

Address Fold Farm, Galley Lane, Barnet, EN5 4RA, +44 (0)208 447 1593, www.lewisoflondon.co.uk // Getting there Free onsite parking, or tube to High Barnet (Northern Line) then bus 107 to the top of Galley Lane (by the Arkley Pub), then a 10–15-minute walk // Hours Daily 10am–5pm // Ages 0+

TIP: Four Seasons Forest School aims to boost self-esteem and promote independence by connecting with the natural world. Sessions are held at Lewis of London.

51_LONDON MUSEUM DOCKLANDS

From pirates to financial traders

Canary Wharf is globally known as a financial district. People in suits whizz about looking important (and they probably are), dashing to meetings or client lunches. When the pandemic struck, the area stood still, with only essential key workers and financial traders heading to the wharf. Coming out of the pandemic, and with a new homeworking system in place, Canary Wharf had to embrace a new direction to reel people back. While still an important part of global finance, it has upped its entertainment offerings for both adults and kids.

Still standing strong despite what 2020 threw at us, nestled below the towering banks above is the London Museum Docklands. Since it opened in 2003, the museum has welcomed thousands of families through its doors. Once inside, it's easy to see why. Wonderfully curated, the museum takes you on a journey of London's dockland history from imports and exports, to the merchants, sailors and pirates of London and what it was like back then. Plus maritime artefacts, a history of the slave trade and treasures from the shores of the Thames. One favourite exhibit is Sailortown, where you wander through alleyways recreating a ramshackle London district.

Mudlarks is a great area for younger kids to go wild! Here they can play with wooden boats and move them along a 3D-model of the River Thames, put on a hard hat and build with giant blocks, zoom in the soft play, lift items on pulleys, and try on an old diver's helmet. The museum offers plentiful immersive learning and fun.

Address No. 1, West India Quay, Hertsmere Road, London, E14 4AL, +44 (0)207 001 9844, www.museumoflondon.org.uk/museum-london-docklands // Getting there Tube to Canary Wharf; DLR to West India Quay // Hours Daily 10am–5pm // Ages 1+

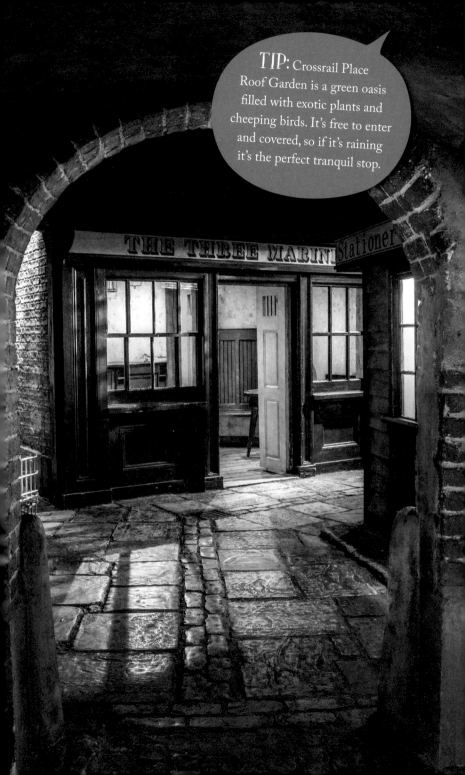

TIP: Crossrail Place Roof Garden is a green oasis filled with exotic plants and cheeping birds. It's free to enter and covered, so if it's raining it's the perfect tranquil stop.

52_ LONDON TRANSPORT MUSEUM

All aboard!

In the heart of Covent Garden you'll find the London Transport Museum, housed in a building once used as part of the famous flower market before it moved to Nine Elms in the 1970s. As you approach the entrance, look up at the original arched Victorian windows.

London is served by an ever-changing transport system with new technologies, route extensions and new lines appearing every few years. The London Transport Museum tells the history of London's transport network through the years. It houses real vehicles including an omnibus, steam train, Routemaster bus, tram, London underground train carriage, a taxi and much more – some of which you can actually get onboard! The museum is an Aladdin's cave of history and interactive learning. Children can drive a tube train, play in the All Aboard play zone, which is full of mini vehicles, or enter the Hidden London exhibition to discover some of London's most secret spaces in the Tube network. There is also a great event line-up throughout the year, including a visit from Father Christmas in December.

They also host Early and Evening Explorer Events for families with SEN. Sensory bags are also available for little explorers to borrow. These include sensory objects and resources such as interactive items and a focus on some of the vehicles in the museum, which in turn connect learners to the collection.

> **TIP:** St Paul's Church on the Piazza hosts family events including the annual May Fayre and Puppet Festival.

Entry to the museum is free for under 16s with a paying adult, and the adult visit is valid for one year, so you can visit over and over again!

Address Covent Garden, East Piazza, London, WC2E 7BB, +44 (0)343 222 5000, www.ltmuseum.co.uk // Getting there Tube to Covent Garden (Piccadilly Line) // Hours Daily 10am–6pm // Ages 0+

53_ LONDON ZOO

A roaring day out

Regent's Park is a charming 410-acre green space. It is also home to the world's oldest scientific zoo, London Zoo. Housing animals from around the globe, the zoo makes a fantastic day out, or evening if you fancy spending a night in one of the zoo lodges. Do away with the alarm clock as you'll hear the roar from an Asiatic lion to kick off your day. As well as lions, you can see a silverback gorilla, lemurs, storks, frogs, otters, penguins, sloths, vipers and tarantulas, to name a few. In fact, there are over 10,000 animals to see. To get up close to the animals you can try one of the zoo experiences, such as meet the meerkats and monkeys, or help out as an honorary penguin or tiger keeper.

The set-up of the zoo is wonderfully thought out to give visitors the best experience with each animal. Glassed walls mean you can see the penguins dive and swim under the water. The giraffe house offers an eye-level encounter with the world's tallest land mammal. Kids of all ages are catered for, with specific programmes and activities for toddlers, pre-schoolers, primary and secondary children. From petting pygmy goats, to spending the day as a junior zoo keeper, children will be introduced to the animal world up close, supported by the fantastic zoo team.

Sensory Stories at the Zoo is a wonderful session for babies who will experience the sights, sounds and textures of life under the sea. London Zoo also offers relaxed monthly SEN tours, BSL tours and audio tours for visually impaired visitors.

Address Outer Circle, London, NW1 4SX, +44 (0)344 225 1826, www.londonzoo.org // Getting there Tube to Camden Town (Northern Line) // Hours Daily 10am–6pm (shorter hours during winter months); see website // Ages 0+

TIP: Explore Camden Lock and market and see if you can find the Hans & Gretel shop for a sweet treat.

54_ LONDONER BUSES

Ride an old Routemaster bus

You may have seen the many tourist buses weaving around Central London. But the little-known Londoner Buses run an old Routemaster bus that does the same as the other companies, but at a fraction of the cost and on an original London bus that was built in the 1960s.

Ding, ding! Take a ride on the Heritage Route T15 run by super friendly conductors. You'll journey from Trafalgar Square (bus stop address below) to the Tower of London, calling at Covent Garden, Aldwych, Royal Courts of Justice, Fleet Street, St Paul's Cathedral and Monument along the way. If you catch the first service in the morning, or the last returning service of the day, you'll get to ride over the bridge from and to Waterloo Station. Check out the tip as to where to grab a great breakfast in Waterloo if you were to catch the first service of the day.

As it's a hop-on-hop-off service, you are free to alight at any of the 14 stops to explore the area, then when you are ready to move on, simply head back to the bus stop and wait for your next ride – it shouldn't be too long. It's a great way to explore Central London at your own pace.

> TIP: Grab a full English from 8am Mon–Fri at the Bus Café in the Waterloo Bus Garage, where real bus drivers stop for a cuppa on their break.

The best seats, in my opinion, are on the top deck right at the front of the bus. Sitting here you can look out of the large windows and take in all of the wonderful the sights... and also peep over any walls if you want to be nosey. If you don't want to go upstairs, then head straight for the seats at the front left of the bus where you can even glimpse the bus driver.

Address Bus Stop F, 460 Strand, London, WC2R 0RG, +44 (0)783 503 1471, www.londonerbuses.co.uk // Getting there Tube or train to Charing Cross (Northern and Bakerloo Lines) // Hours See website for current information on timetable // Ages 0+

55__THE LUDOQUIST

Board games for the whole family

Board game fans will love The Ludoquist. This is a great board game café in the centre of Croydon where you can lose a day playing games. They have over 1,000 board games to choose from, suitable from age two plus, so all the family can get involved.

A bit like a casino in Las Vegas, once you are in there, there is no need to leave as they have a café onsite that serves drinks and food. There is nothing better than playing a family game while tucking into a warm pizza and finishing with a syrup sponge with ice cream (healthier options are available)! Parents – don't worry. Beer, wine and cocktails are available too, to help lubricate the game session. And The Ludoquist has just won the famed Blue Ribbon in the Good Food Awards so you know you're in safe hands.

You can also BYOB (bring your own board-game) so if you have a game at home that rarely sees the light of day, you can bring it along and play together, or invite another family and play against each other (save you having to tidy the house for visitors!). And if you find a game you love, you can buy it there or online.

The Ludoquist runs events throughout the year, a popular one being their Dungeons and Dragons kids' sessions for ages 11+. This is a fabulous hub for boardgame lovers and better still, it cuts down on screentime, which we are all guilty of overdoing these days. Booking a visit is highly recommended as it's a super popular place to be, and one that gets very busy at weekends and during school holidays. Dogs are welcome too.

Address 63–67 High Street, Croydon, CR0 1QE, +44 (0)203 011 2295, www.theludoquist.com // Getting there Train to East Croydon // Hours Mon–Thu 3–10pm, Fri 2–11pm, Sat 11am–11pm & Sun 11am–8pm (extended hours during school holidays) // Ages 2+

TIP: The Museum of Croydon situated at the clocktower offers a fascinating insight into local history, with collections and spaces that represent every aspect of Croydon.

56_MARKFIELD

A pumphouse and a princess

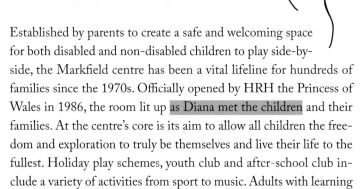

Established by parents to create a safe and welcoming space for both disabled and non-disabled children to play side-by-side, the Markfield centre has been a vital lifeline for hundreds of families since the 1970s. Officially opened by HRH the Princess of Wales in 1986, the room lit up as Diana met the children and their families. At the centre's core is its aim to allow all children the freedom and exploration to truly be themselves and live their life to the fullest. Holiday play schemes, youth club and after-school club include a variety of activities from sport to music. Adults with learning difficulties love the social club, as well as the uber popular Friday Club Night, which is on until 9pm.

While the services for children are so vital, it's imperative that their adults are supported too. Markfield offers a fantastic series of services for families, giving them power to build social networks and receive support from the local community. Regular events open to everyone include Adventure Playground (drop in on Saturdays) and the Family Club (second Saturday of the month during term time) where children can play on the zip wire and swing on the swings. The event even includes a light lunch and on occasion a bonfire.

TIP: The Markfield Beam Engine and Museum is just next door.

What makes this centre unique is its setting in an old Victorian pump house, refurbished of course, adding to the character and history of Markfield. The centre has ingrained itself in the community over the years, and it certainly isn't going anywhere soon.

Address Markfield Road, London, N15 4RB, +44 (0)208 800 4134, www.markfield.org.uk // Getting there Train to Tottenham Hale or tube to Seven Sisters (Victoria Line) // Hours Office: Mon–Fri 9.30am–5pm; see website for events and activities timetable // Ages 0+

57_MAYFIELD LAVENDER FARM

Is it really in London?

'But it's not in London' some people might screech. Well, actually it is! Head to the outskirts of the London Borough of Sutton (yep, it's a London borough) during the summer months and inhale the divine smell of lavender. The purple hues of the striking plants lead off into the distance, making for a wonderful walk.

Set in an original Victorian lavender field, the current 25-acre farm was re-established in 2002 and opened to the public in 2008. The beauty of this field has seen visitor numbers rise each year, with people from across the globe making their way to the purple haven. There is even an old red London telephone box in the field, which really pops against the purple backdrop. As well as the beauty of the lavender, the farm also sells its own produce in the onsite café. You can sample lavender lemonade alongside some lavender shortbread in the outside seating area overlooking the vibrant plants. They also have items to take home such as lavender gin liquor, body lotion, candles and essential oils. And check out their Top Tips on using lavender for everything from insect bites to a headache remedy.

They also sell honey. As you take a stroll through the fields you may notice some bees buzzing about collecting nectar to make honey. While they don't have their own hives, the honey sold at the farm is from local bee hives just up the road on the Surrey Downs.

Be careful, as lavender is known to improve sleep, so try not to drift off in this tranquil setting.

Address 1 Carshalton Road, Banstead, SM7 3JA, +44 (0)750 387 7707, www.mayfieldlavender.com // Getting there Sat Nav postcode SM7 3JA; by train Victoria to Purley Station, then bus 166 outside Tesco to Oaks Park // Hours Farm opening seasonal, so check website // Ages 0+

TIP: Gamers unite!
Belong Sutton is a great
place for gamers to take
part in tournaments,
or casual gaming.

58_THE MERCERS TREASURE WALK

Treasures hidden in plain sight

The Yards in Covent Garden is a traffic free oasis of calm. You can enjoy a coffee while your little one toddles about, or grab a spot of lunch on one of the restaurant balconies overlooking the courtyard. Opening in recent years, The Yards is a great addition to the area.

There's plenty to offer for families at The Yards. Dine at a choice of worldwide cuisines, grab a special gelato for your dog from Badiani, have your nails done at Townhouse, shop for a beautiful map at Stanfords, take a dance class at the world-renowned Pineapple Dance Studios or an art class at the London Graphic Centre. Behind here on Mercer Street you can see a super vibrant mural reading 'Creativity is in all of us' – a fitting tag for the back of an art shop.

Outside of Stanfords, the extremely talented international artist and cartographer Adam Dant has created a huge map of Covent Garden that includes people, quotes and history. Do you recognise any of the places you can see?

On the wall in Mercer Walk you'll discover The Mercers Treasure Walk map directing you to various hidden treasures dotted around. The tiny sculptures are encased in glass, and represent various points in history. One example is a golden sheep with golden lambs to represent England's main export prior to the Industrial Revolution. Follow the directions on the map to find the little treasures hidden in walls and in the ground.

Can you find them all? You'll have to look hard as there may be a plant or other obstacle in the way!

Address Mercer Walk, London, WC2H 9QP // Getting there Tube to Covent Garden (Piccadilly Line) // Hours Accessible 24 hours // Ages 4+

The murder of Thomas Becket in Canterbury Cathedral, 29th December 1170

Thomas Becket was born *c.1120* in Cheapside in the City of London, in a house where Mercers' Hall now stands. Only three years after his dramatic murder, the Pope canonised him. St Thomas's cult spread rapidly throughout Europe, making Canterbury one of the most important pilgrimage destinations. The Knights of St Thomas, an order founded twenty years after his death, acquired the site of their patron saint's birth in the 1220s and built a monastery named the Hospital of St Thomas of Acon. The Mercers' Company met there from the 14th Century and, after its dissolution in 1538, purchased the site. Following the Great Fire of London in 1666, Mercers' Hall was rebuilt on the site where the monastery had stood.

TIP: Fancy a dip? The Oasis Sports Centre has Central London's only public heated outdoor swimming pool.

59_MERTON ABBEY MILLS

A wheel powered... wheel!

Set in the grounds of a former textile factory, Merton Abbey Mills is a delightful spot to explore. In previous years Liberty's, famed for its unique designs, had their popular ranges of fabrics for furniture and clothes made at the factory here, which were subsequently sold in their Regent's Street store.

At Merton Abbey Mills, on the edge of the River Wandle, you'll find a charming and fully working waterwheel. Families can enter the old Wheelhouse building and see how it all works. Of the almost 100 watermills that stood along the River Wandle, this is one of only four remaining, and is the only one in full working order. This wheel was also used by Liberty's to rinse the gum (a thickening agent used for textile printing) off their printed silk. The Wheelhouse is free to visit and houses a gallery and pottery workshops. Interestingly, the working wheel is actually used to turn the potter's wheel.

TIP: Walk along the River Wandle to Deen City Farm, for an urban farm with an educational focus and some rare British animal breeds.

As well as learning the fascinating history set against the gentle whooshing sound of the water being churned by the wheel, you can explore an array of craft stalls, enjoy kids' theatre and discover eateries from across the world such as the Caribbean, Thailand, Belgium and Argentina. You can even sit in a pirate ship while you eat a steak.

If that isn't enough, The William Morris Pub has a lovely outside terrace overlooking the water, and on certain dates it hosts a kids' table where mini punters can enjoy crafting and activities while their adults relax with a drink.

THE WHEELHOUSE

The unique bespoke waterwheel dates from
c.1860 and is London's only working example.
Liberty used it to drive spools to rinse
the silk after dumming and printing.
The water powered potters wheel
is also unique. The building is Grade II listed.

MERTON ABBEY MILLS

THE WHEELHOUSE
POTTERY
www.stephenllewellynpottery.co.uk

WHEELHOUSE
ART

lino cutting and printing
workshops weekly
Booking essential. To book
& for more details call
07812 131360 or go to
www.wheelhouseart.co.uk

Wandle
Heritage

Address Watermill Way, London,
SW19 2RD, www.mertonabbeymills.org.uk //
Getting there Just off the A24; tube
to Colliers Wood (Northern Line) //
Hours Daily 8am–6pm // Ages 5+

60_MICHELIN HOUSE

From tyres to oysters

It was built in 1911 by the Michelin Tyre Company as their UK headquarters. Look up and you'll see stained-glass windows that incorporate vibrant colours and an image of The Michelin Man (or Bibendum, shortened to Bib). They double up as advertising to promote the brand. When the Michelin brothers created the brand, they opted for a mascot made of tyres, which back then were white, and so this iconic tyre man was born. Look closely at the image of Bib and you'll see he is holding a drink filled with broken glass. This image was accompanied with the slogan 'Nunc est Bibendum', which translates as 'now is the time to drink'. The broken glass symbolises the strength of the tyres and that they won't puncture easily. Running along the exterior of the building you'll see tiled images depicting famous motor races, such as Paris to Madrid in 1903.

Now step inside the front of the building, which houses Claude Bosi's two Michelin-starred restaurant (yep, not just tyres; they created the restaurant starring system too) and a famous flower stall. This was once the tyre fitting bay. Customers would hang around waiting for the job to be done, so it was decided to add an eatery. Ground level is an oyster bar, again the walls adorned with images of races, and upstairs is the fancy restaurant where you will find one of a kind Michelin memorabilia. You'll also get a closer look at the stained glass. Michelin still runs at the heart of this building – even the butter dishes have Bib sitting on the edge.

Address 81 Fulham Road, London, SW3 6RD, +44 (0)207 581 5817, www.claudebosi.com // Getting there Tube to South Kensington (Piccadilly, Circle & District Lines) // Hours Viewable from the outside 24 hours; bookings for Claude Bosi at Bibendum by telephone or via the website // Ages 5+

TIP: The Natural History Museum is a must when in South Kensington.

61__ THE MOSAIC HOUSE

Anarchy through art

Home to artist Carrie Reichardt, The Mosaic House is one of the most impressive residential homes in London. It even has its own Instagram account. Over 20 years in the making, and using her own house in Chiswick that has been in the family since the 1940s as the canvas, Carrie has entirely covered the house from front to back in a wonderfully intricate mosaic design. While Carrie was the driving force behind the project, the finished piece is an amalgamation of artists from around the world.

A self-proclaimed anarchist and activist, Carrie started the project after wanting to create a piece of work that was completely uncensored and that she was in control of. With statements such as 'I'm an artist, your rules don't apply' and 'I rebel therefore we exist', the artwork is a vivid statement of works with a plethora of messages. Head round to the back of the house to see works in commemoration to Luis Ramirez, a prisoner on death row whom Carrie became good friends with. Look up to see *The Great Wave off Kanagawa* with London landmarks submerged by water thanks to global warming.

At the front of the house, you'll see the disappearing Cheshire Cat from *Alice in Wonderland*. Actually, there are two; can you find the second one before it vanishes? Look closely and see if you can spot the 23 eyeballs dotted about. In front is parked a black cab adorned with petrol-coloured tiles, and the interior has been decorated too. There's even a passenger in the back. Now, where could he be off to?

TIP: Chiswick House and Gardens offers beautiful grounds to explore as well as special events and family activities.

Address 4–6 Fairlawn Grove, London, W4 5EL, www.carriereichardt.com // Getting there Tube to Chiswick Park (District Line) // Hours Viewable from the outside only // Ages 0+

62_MUDCHUTE PARK AND FARM

In the shadow of Canary Wharf

A staple of the East London community for decades, Mudchute has embedded itself fully. As the surrounding area grew taller with big global banks creating a New York-style financial district just around the corner, Mudchute fought and survived a proposed redevelopment of high-rise building on the land. In 1977, farm animals and horses were introduced alongside trees and flowers to enhance what was affectionately known as the People's Park. The acre and a half of land has so much to offer to anyone of any age. Entry is free (with a suggested donation) and the offerings are vast.

Here at one of the largest city farms in Europe, you can get up close and meet animals including chickens, rabbits, goats, llamas and sheep. There is also a young farmers' programme where children can learn about life on the farm, as well as an afterschool club, arts and crafts, and Mudchute Play – a child-led play session in the farm's courtyard. Donkey rides are popular, as are the special events hosted throughout the year. There is also a World War II exhibition that tells the role of Mudchute during the Blitz. You can make a day of it and take a picnic to eat there. Cycling is a great way to visit Mudchute as you can safely park up and explore the farm, and once you are done you can mosey on to the river and enjoy a ride along the traffic free Thames Path.

I'll leave you with a fun fact: the word 'Mudchute' arose from the previous use of the land. Mud dredged from local Millwall Docks was dumped here, thus becoming Mudchute.

TIP: Folly House Beach is just along the river and makes for a fun little stop on a sunny day. You can walk on the pebbled beach and take in views of the O₂ Centre.

Address Pier Street, London, E14 3HP,
+44 (0)207 515 5901, www.mudchute.org //
Getting there DLR to Mudchute // Hours
Farm open daily 9am–4pm; park daily
dawn–dusk // Ages 1+

63_ NATIONAL COVID MEMORIAL WALL

A wall of love

Can you remember what you were doing in March 2020? That was the year that changed the world as we knew it. While we have all managed to modify how we live, and to an extent have returned to normality, the Covid-19 pandemic is part of modern history, a history that we all lived through.

As you read this book you may well be one of the parents who had to give birth alone in hospital, or were not allowed into the hospital to be with your partner, so were waiting anxiously outside for any news on your new born baby. Or perhaps you are a child who couldn't see your friends for what felt like an eternity! We each have our own stories to tell from this difficult time.

Stretching 500 yards along the south side of the River Thames, just outside of St Thomas' Hospital opposite the Houses of Parliament, is the beautiful National Covid Memorial Wall displaying over 220,000 individually hand-painted red hearts. Each heart represents someone from the UK who was loved and lost during the pandemic. The wall is a place of solace and hope for all of us, young and old. Take a moment to read the beautiful messages written in the hearts. The official memorial wall website states: 'If you have lost a loved-one to Covid-19 in the UK, visitors to the Wall are very welcome to add their own dedication. We ask that one heart is taken only, as each heart represents one UK life lost.'

TIP: You can see Big Ben from here, so how about climbing up the 334-step spiral stairwell to the top and standing behind the clockface? Be warned, you must book in advance as it's very popular!

Address National Covid Memorial
Wall, London, SE1 3FT,
www.nationalcovidmemorialwall.org //
Getting there Tube to Westminster
(Jubilee, District and Circle Lines) //
Hours Accessible 24 hours // Ages 3+

64_ NEAL'S YARD CLOCK

Time to water the flowers

This was a favourite of mine as a child, the Neal's Yard Water Clock. I'd stand and watch the orange float rise to the top of the tube as it filled with water released from a tank on the rooftop, then as the clock struck the hour, water would flow down setting off chimes while little people watered their flowers. The best bit was the small figure on the left who would turn and pour water onto us and the pavement below. As children, we found it hilarious.

While the figure on the left no longer squirts water, presumably due to complaints from unaware passers-by, it's well worth a couple of minutes of your time to see it in action if you happen to be on Short's Gardens on the hour.

The clock was created by Tim Hunkin and Andy Plant, and adorns the front of a building that is currently a fancy restaurant. To the left you will see a small walkway leading into Neal's Yard. This vibrant traffic free courtyard is a burst of colour and creativity. Here you can dine, shop and treat yourself to a makeover! But more interestingly the yard is home to one of London's many famous blue plaques. Can you find it?

Blue plaques celebrate the connection between famous people and people who are experts in their field throughout history with the buildings in which they lived or worked. However, the one in Neal's Yard is one of the plaques connected to a 'person who doesn't exist'! It is in fact for Monty Python, a very famous British comedy troupe, who used part of the building as their recording and editing studio.

> **TIP:** Seven Dials Market is a foody haven. Offering kids' menus for each cuisine, they also have child-friendly events throughout the year.

136

Address 21–25 Short's Gardens, London, WC2H 9AS // Getting there Tube to Covent Garden (Piccadilly Line) // Hours Accessible 24 hours // Ages 2+

65_NEASDEN TEMPLE

God's body is a temple

Neasden Temple, or BAPS Shri Swaminarayan Mandir, is a haven for Hindu worship, and is quite frankly breathtaking. It would quite easily stop you in your tracks should you stumble across it unawares. Showcasing Hindu art and architecture, the intricate white stone masterpiece was hand carved in India. The temple was shipped to England in a whopping 26,300 individually numbered pieces. Constructed like a giant 3D puzzle by expert artisans and hundreds of volunteers, on completion it received a Guinness World Record for being the largest Hindu temple outside of India.

Dedicated to its principal deity Bhagwan Swaminarayan, the temple is a place for celebration and prayer, and is enjoyed by the whole community. Upon arrival you are greeted by a huge golden statue of His Holiness Pramukh Swami Maharaj, who was a great religious teacher and the creator of Neasden Temple. His golden presence is accompanied by two beautiful elephants in full decorated costume. Based on a tradition going back hundreds of years, the Mandir is a sacred place with components of the temple representing God's body. Look up and you'll see the gold kalashes representing the head of God; the flags symbolise hair, and so on down to the foundations, which represent God's feet. Once inside this spiritual sanctuary, you'll see more of the carved stone, giving details of every aspect of the Mandir from the first foundation to the dedication ceremony.

Neasden Temple is a peaceful space of serenity and connection with the divine.

Address Pramukh Swami Road, Neasden, London, NW10 8HW,
+44 (0)208 965 2651, www.londonmandir.baps.org //
Getting there Train or tube to Neasden (Jubilee Line) //
Hours Daily 9am–6pm (check website for dress code) // Ages 6+

TIP: Shayona Restaurant serves up scrumptious Sattvic vegetarian cuisine that is consistent with Swaminarayan dietary requirements, including a 'This isn't what you think!' curry.

66_THE OLD OPERATING THEATRE MUSEUM

Watch a live surgery, Victorian style!

If the thought of modern-day surgery makes you queasy, then how they performed operations back in the day will make you positively sick! The Old Operating Theatre Museum is an extraordinary experience. Grossness aside, this is a fascinating and educational space that will leave you thankful that you are here today and not in need of medical assistance 150 years ago. The surgical and medical advancements since then are mind-blowing.

Enter the oldest surviving surgical theatre in Europe situated in the attic of St Thomas' Church in a former herb garret that had been bricked up until 1956. To access the attic you must climb a narrow spiral staircase of 52 steps. While they do not have a public lift, there is a small lift for visitors in need of assistance.

Once ascended, you will have access to the surgical theatre where up to 150 medical students at a time would have assembled to learn how to perform surgical procedures. Today, you can book to take your seat in the Victorian Operating Theatre where you will learn about surgical procedures of the time, and even more horrifyingly, how they did them pre the arrival of anaesthesia and antiseptics. You'll see saws, sawdust and all.

As well as general admission, throughout the year the museum hosts family workshops and activities, particularly during school holidays. The museum also offers British Sign Language tours.

Address 9a St Thomas' Street, London, SE1 9RY, +44 (0)207 118 2679, www.oldoperatingtheatre.com // Getting there Tube or train to London Bridge (Northern and Jubilee Lines) // Hours Thu–Sun 10.30am–5pm // Ages 8+

TIP: For wonderful views across London, head up to the Sky Garden just on the other side of London Bridge.

67_PARSLOES PARK PLAY AREA

'The Flamboyance of Flamingos'

Playgrounds across the UK can be dreary places. Which is a shame, as they are such an important part of childhood playtime and – like it or not – adults' time too. Create London and the London Borough of Barking & Dagenham decided to do away with a drab old Dagenham playground and commissioned the extraordinarily talented British-Nigerian multidisciplinary artist and designer Yinka Ilori MBE, to add fun and vibrancy to Parsloes Park Play Area, thus resulting in the effervescent creation of 'The Flamboyance of Flamingos'.

While the use of flamingos seems entertaining, there is a story behind it. A flock of these exotic birds used to live freely in the park. It's hard to imagine sitting on a park bench with your packed lunch only to have flamingos casually pootle by. Now, you'd head to a zoo to see these elegant pink feathered creatures. What's lovely about this playground is that the artist drew inspiration from the area, and bringing flamingos back is such an endearing touch. Children will be amazed to think flamingos really were here in the park and that's what I love – the mash-up of carefree enjoyment that the playground offers, mixed with local history so kids can learn while they play and appreciate what's around them.

Enthusiastically running around, children have fun on the multi-coloured apparatus, including a flamingo roundabout. The basketball court is designed with vibrant colours and a giant floral design, giving a new engaging way to play as the exuberant design runs throughout.

Address Ivy Walk, Dagenham, RM9 5RX // Getting there Tube to Becontree (District Line) // Hours Mon–Fri 8am–4pm, Sat 8am–7pm, Sun 8am–6.30pm // Ages 0+

TIP: Future, Barking & Dagenham Youth Zone, is a fantastic hub of activities for aspiring chefs, filmmakers, artists, boxers, dancers and more, all housed under one roof.

68_PEPYS PARK

Sit on a real cannon

Pepys Park is one of our favourite hidden gems. On the Thames Path (Route 4 if you are a keen cyclist) sits a fantastic little playground. It has all the usual wants for such a place; slides, swings, climbing frames, and not only is it traffic free, it's not even near a busy road so the air is as fresh as the River Thames can provide. A highlight for many kids visiting the playground are the two cannons that line up against the Thames wall and are aimed over the river at some quite innocent looking abodes. Children climb and role play with the historical objects. When we first visited here it was purely by chance on a walk from Waterloo to Greenwich along the river (quite a walk!). It was a beautiful sunny day and Pepys Park seemed the perfect stop for a short break. From the top of the small hill, you not only hop on the slide, there's also a great view across the river towards Canary Wharf.

Just a few steps from the playground you'll find Pepys Community Library. This wonderful resource centre offers workshops and events each month. The bookshop has a collection of pre-loved books, DVDs, CDs and even the odd VHS or record. Items for sale have all been donated, and funds raised from each sale go towards keeping the onsite library open, so it's a great reason for you to have a clear out and make a donation, as well as potentially picking up a little treasure!

Pepys Park is of course named after Samuel Pepys, the diarist who captured the essence of London at a time long before TikTok influencers.

Address 61 Millard Road, London, SE8 3GB // Getting there Train to Surrey Quays or Deptford // Hours Accessible 24 hours // Ages 0+

TIP: Head along the river to Greenland Dock to see dockside townhouses built in the 1990s and have a bite to eat at The Moby Dick while watching water sports in action.

69_THE PHILPOT LANE MICE

A cheesy fight

There are mice in London, we know that. We may even see them scurrying along the tracks of the underground, or dashing along a pavement wall to avoid being spotted. But we don't really consider them to be above our heads. Wandering along an outwardly normal little street in Monument, you may want to look up. On Philpot Lane there is an interesting sight.

Look up and you'll see two little mice fighting over a piece of delicious cheddar (I presume) cheese. Creating humour and intrigue, there are a few theories as to how the hungry pair came to adorn the side of this building. One such theory is that the carving depicts the little rodent rascals who would regularly steal workmen's lunches while the building was under construction many years ago. Another more sinister version is that of two workmen who fought over a 'missing lunch'; one thought the other had pinched it. While arguing on the scaffolding, their hangry, boisterous struggle resulted in the pair falling to the ground, never to eat a packed lunch again. After later finding out that mice, not their workmate, had stolen the lunch, their colleagues had two mice fighting over cheese carved in memory of the late workmen. Thank goodness for the invention of mouse-proof Tupperware.

There are approximately half a million mice living in the London underground network alone – that's two for every resident of Westminster. While they aren't always easy to see, just be mindful that they are around and always on the hunt for cheese, even the stinky stuff!

Address 23 Eastcheap, London, EC3M 1DE // Getting there Tube to Monument (Central and District Lines) // Hours Accessible 24 hours // Ages 4+

TIP: St Dunstan-in-the-East Church Garden is a beautiful tranquil spot, perfect for a little picnic or to bask in the sun in a stunning ivy-draped ruin.

70_ POLICE OFFICER BOLLARD

'Ello 'ello 'ello, what do we have 'ere then?

Standing guard outside what used to be the Gerald Road Police Station in Belgravia is PC Broxap, a police officer-shaped bollard. On duty 24 hours a day, he is dressed in a uniform resembling the old-style bobbies who gave the force its nickname 'boys in blue'.

The police station opened in 1846 on what was then called Cottage Row. Over the years, many a criminal was brought here. One of the most notorious was Ronnie Biggs, the great train robber, who once spent a night here.

The police station wasn't just known for its notorious criminals; it was quite the celebrity itself! Gerald Road Police Station made the press on multiple occasions for the awards it used to win, most notably the Westminster Gardeners Guild Cup two years running for the floral displays that adorned the frontage. Belgravia has been full of green fingers throughout the years, and to this day they celebrate Belgravia in Bloom each year.

Situated in one of London's richest areas, this police station was local to many important people, not just Londoners. At the time of its proposed closure, the station's patrol zone covered many diplomatic premises that represented different countries and global organisations. With this in mind, the question of its closure was debated in the House of Commons, but in 1993 the police station was closed for good.

Now converted into a residential property, there is a blue plaque above the main entrance referencing the building's original use. Would you live in an old police station?

Address 7 Gerald Road, London, SW1W 9EH // Getting there Tube to Sloane Square (Circle and District Lines) or train or tube to Victoria (Victoria, Circle and District Lines) // Hours Accessible 24 hours // Ages 3+

TIP: Eccleston Yards is a vibrant traffic-free space filled with eateries, alfresco seating, colourful murals and a big screen to watch sport and family-friendly films for free during the summer months.

71_THE POSTAL MUSEUM

Travel via Mail Rail!

Who was England's monarch when the postal service began? A) Queen Victoria, B) George I, C) Henry VIII.

It might surprise you to learn that the postal service has in fact been in action for more than 500 years, since the reign of Henry VIII. The then king asked Sir Brian Tuke to set up a national postal network for the use of the king's court. It wasn't until the reign of Charles I that the network was opened for public use.

Situated in Clerkenwell, the Postal Museum is a fascinating place to discover the postal journey over the last 500 years. With over 60,000 objects, a vast collection of records, and inside knowledge of how the postal service is run, you might look at the humble envelope you pop into the letter box without a second thought in a whole new light. The museum is also built on the original site of the Mail Rail, a subterranean network of trains transporting mail right beneath our feet as we'd wander, unaware, through the streets of London above. For over 75 years, this subterranean postal rail service was a vital means of communication transport. Avoiding London's congested streets, the Mail Rail was a swift service delivering all letters and packages to sorting offices across the city.

TIP: Novelty Automation houses a collection of satirical home-made arcade machines guaranteed to amuse!

Though the service was terminated in 2003, it has since been brought back to life, and you can now take a ride on the Mail Rail's miniature train, which is 70 feet deep in the original tunnels. They also host monthly guided walking tours of these historical tunnels for those aged 12 years and over.

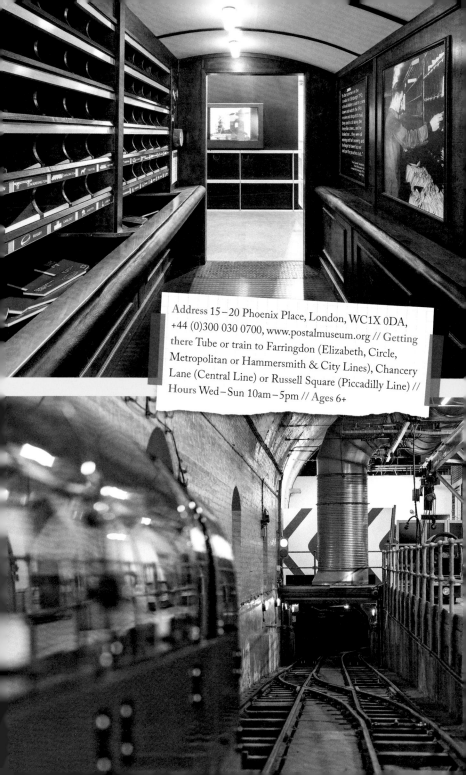

Address 15–20 Phoenix Place, London, WC1X 0DA, +44 (0)300 030 0700, www.postalmuseum.org // Getting there Tube or train to Farringdon (Elizabeth, Circle, Metropolitan or Hammersmith & City Lines), Chancery Lane (Central Line) or Russell Square (Piccadilly Line) // Hours Wed–Sun 10am–5pm // Ages 6+

72_ PUPPET THEATRE BARGE

A visit with no strings attached

London is brimming with theatre venues. With clusters of historical spots in the West End, the Globe Theatre on the Thames, an open-air theatre in Regent's Park, the choice of venues is vast. So how about a trusty 1920s log barge that has been converted into a 50-seat theatre? The Puppet Theatre Barge is a truly unique live performance venue that has been putting on great family-friendly puppetry shows for over 40 years.

Step aboard and head below deck (mind your head!) where you'll be instantly immersed in the magical land of puppetry. Venture past old retired puppets from around the world that hang proudly along the wall. Once seated, a bell chimes indicating the show is about to commence. What makes the experience one of a kind is not just the venue, but the craftsmanship, technique and lighting design. This venue is one of the last marionette (string puppet) theatres in the country. The puppets are hand crafted and have neutral facial expressions to allow for a full range of emotions to be conveyed. Detailed lighting design and precise movements from the hidden puppeteer bring the characters' expressions to life. The puppets move across the stage with a lightness and grace that must take years to master.

> **TIP:** All aboard the Waterbus for a 45-minute discovery of the Regent's Canal taking you from Little Venice to Camden Market.

The Puppet Theatre Barge travels along the canal throughout the year, which ensures further reach to families along the waterway and beyond. London bases include Little Venice and Richmond. The full events line up is on their website. It's a must visit with the kids in London!

Address Opposite 35 Blomfield Road, London, W9 2PF, +44 (0)207 249 6876, www.puppetbarge.com // **Getting there** Tube to Warwick Avenue (Bakerloo Line) // **Hours** Check website for times // **Ages 4+**

73_ QUEEN ELIZABETH I STATUE

How can a statue make money?

Fleet Street has been famous for printing and publishing since the start of the 16th century. You may recognise the term 'Fleet Street' used in reference to the British National Press. This isn't all Fleet Street is famous for. The church, St Dunstan-in-the-West, possesses an intriguing statue with a bountiful tale.

The church itself, once octagonal in shape before being rebuilt, hosts free lunchtime recitals and is open for prayer and services. From the outside you'll see a clock known to be the first clock in London to have a minute hand installed. Behind this are two giants, Gog and Magog, the guardians of London, who chime the bells with clubs, and turn their heads. On the façade you'll also notice a statue of Queen Elizabeth I. Originally in Ludgate, this figurine was carved in the 1580s during the queen's reign. Ludgate was demolished in the 18th century, so the statue was brought to St Dunstan's and has been here ever since.

But this isn't just any old statue of Queen Elizabeth I. This one has its own income! Fretful that the statue would fall into disrepair, Dame Millicent Fawcett, a political activist and writer who also became the leader of the National Union of Women's Suffrage Societies, left the statue a significant sum. The money was to be used towards the cleaning and repair of the statue in perpetuity. While back in the day the significant sum of £700 would have lasted a while, I'm not sure how much of it will remain with today's repair rates.

> **TIP:** Pop round the corner to the Old Bank of England and hop aboard the stationary red Routemaster bus. They have a yummy kids' menu!

PAROCHIAL SCHOOLS.
S.T DUNSTAN IN THE WEST.
A.D. 1839.

The Statue of
QUEEN ELIZABETH
formerly stood on the West side of LUDGATE.
That Gate being taken down in 1760 to open the Street,
was given by the CITY to S.R FRANCIS GOSLING K.N.T.
ALDERMAN of this WARD who caused it to

Address 186a Fleet Street,
London, EC4A 2AT // Getting
there Tube to Temple (Circle
and District Lines) // Hours
Accessible 24 hours // Ages 5+

74_REAL TIME

A man trapped in a clock

London is home to thousands of clocks, most famous being on the Elizabeth Tower and known as Big Ben. This is actually the name of the bell that chimes each hour, not the clock itself. Another is Little Ben in Victoria whose time is permanently set to Daylight Saving Time (DST) making the time correct for France in winter and for the UK in the summer. There's the Fortnum and Mason clock, as well as the clock on Horse Guards Parade where a black mark at 2pm indicates the time that King Charles I was executed in January 1649 – a cheery reminder. Shell Mex house on The Strand has a large clock facing over the Thames that you may have seen on TV in the background of news reports or daytime TV shows.

Now, imagine being stuck in a clock, 24 hours a day for all eternity. In Paddington you'll find a man who is doing just that. Okay, it's not a real man, but it does make you think. *Real Time* by Dutch artist Maarten Baas showcases a digital man inside a large clock. He is constantly working away to ensure the clock hands tell the correct time by drawing them, rubbing them out and re-drawing them to the next minute. Look closely and you'll even see him peering out looking at you. The man is dressed in a 19th-century three-piece suit as a reference to the time of Brunel, in a nod to Paddington Station, which Brunel designed.

Can you think of any more clocks? Take a look around as you meander through the streets of London. You'll be amazed at how many you'll see!

Address 50 Eastbourne Terrace, London, W2 6LG // Getting there Train or tube to Paddington (Elizabeth, District and Circle Lines) // Hours Accessible 24 hours // Ages 5+

TIP: Merchant Square is a lovely waterside spot with a water maze, rolling bridge and many family-friendly events.

156

75_THE ROYAL EXCHANGE

A home for trading stocks

As you exit Bank underground station, you'll emerge in front of a building that exudes grandeur and presence. That is, of course, if you leave the station via the correct exit as there are 16 of them, more than any other London Underground station. It's like a rabbit warren, so always be early when heading to Bank if you have an appointment, as trying to exit can take up valuable minutes. Once above ground, eventually, you'll find The Royal Exchange.

Now a luxury retail shopping and dining destination, The Royal Exchange first opened its doors in 1566 as London's first purpose-built centre for trading stocks. The building was opened in 1571 by Queen Elizabeth I, who granted it the royal title. Like most of the city, the building was destroyed in the Great Fire of London in 1666. Merchants and brokers returned to the rebuilt Exchange in 1669. Yikes, fire strikes again! In 1838 the building burned to the ground for a second time. The one before you today was opened in 1844, and they take fire safety very seriously.

Throughout the year you can visit the building and see the magnificent architecture inside, as well as dining in one of the family-friendly eateries such as Fortnum & Mason or The Libertine, and even look out for one of the many installations in and around the building. Previous years have seen a Darth Fisher (a fishing Darth Vader) installation by Dutch artist Streetart Frankey, and the Tusk Rhino Trail outside the front of the building, part of a London-wide art installation.

TIP: London Mithraeum Bloomberg SPACE showcases the remains of a Roman temple.

Address Royal Exchange, London, EC3V 3LL, +44 (0)203 861 6500, www.theroyalexchange.co.uk // Getting there Tube or DLR to Bank (Central, Northern and Waterloo & City Lines) // Hours Mon–Fri 7.30am–10pm // Ages 8+

76_RUISLIP LIDO BEACH

A hidden village under the water

Kick off your shoes, lay out your towel, fill your bucket with sand and settle in for a day at Ruislip Lido Beach. Set in north-west London, this splendid family-friendly base has lots to offer. You'll find a beach playground with pirate ships and a crocodile (not a real one, obvs!), a splash park to cool off, a Walk the Planets trail, ancient woodland walks, café and changing facilities. As well as this, you can hop aboard the Ruislip Lido Railway, which includes accessible seating, for a two-mile ride around the lake.

As you relax on the beach, take a look out into the centre of the lake, for something covert lurks beneath. Dug in 1811 as a reservoir, what was here before then? The Grand Junction Canal company wanted to build a feeder for the nearby canal, and a reservoir, so they got out their cheque books and demanded the residents leave their humble abodes on the land. While these were being demolished, the  reservoir began to fill, and water engulfed the remainder of the houses, submerging them into the depths of the cold water never to be seen again… or so it was thought. In 1990 a severe drought hit and revealed the bed of the reservoir. Locals were astonished to see the outline of a building. They dug a little deeper and discovered the remains of walls from the old houses. The drought ended, water returned and the lost village was covered up again.

If you want to go looking for them, I'd advise against it. Swimming is forbidden in the lido. Best to stick with the splash park to cool off.

TIP: Duck Pond Market held at Manor Farm is home to locally made food, art, gifts, vintage items and homewares set against the backdrop of live performances. The market is held on certain days each month.

Address Reservoir Road, Ruislip, HA4 7TX, +44 (0)189 555 6000, www.ruisliplido.com // **Getting there** Tube to Ruislip (Metropolitan and Piccadilly Lines) // **Hours** Open daily 9am, but closing times vary throughout the year, so check website // **Ages** 0+

77_SHEPHERDESS WALK MOSAICS

A modern story told in pictures

You'll need to keep your eyes peeled for this small, unobtrusive entrance snuck between two terraced houses. Enter the short passageway and head to the end where you'll emerge into a delightful hidden courtyard. The mosaic in Shepherdess Walk is a fascinating piece of work. Usually we see mosaics depicting patterns, stories, history and artefacts of times gone by. Here, however, you will see a modern-day reflection of how we have lived in recent times. While the design is in the style of traditional mosaics with pastel colours and soft edges, the modern content is quite remarkable. Of course, the mosaic also includes a nod to the roots of the area with a section showing the shepherdesses and sheep that gave the area its name.

Depicting Hackney in 2012, the large artwork covers various local areas through the seasons. You'll spot a boy skateboarding in spring, a child buying ice cream in summer, a man with a leaf blower in autumn, and a mother on her smartphone in winter. And that's just cherry picking a few items – there is so much more to it. The more you look, the more you see.

What makes this celebration of our modern day living so special is that the piece was designed and created by mosaicist Tessa Hunkin, who led the idea and fruition of the project, and got together 150 volunteers from the local community. Within these volunteers were people from Lifeline Works, for those struggling with substance abuse, who also contributed time to bringing this masterpiece to life. It's well worth a visit.

Address Between 135 and 137 Shepherdess Walk, London, N1 7QA // Getting there Tube to Angel (Northern Line) // Hours Accessible 24 hours (when gates closed, enter through park on your left) // Ages 4+

TIP: Bob the cat has been immortalised on a bench not far from here. The story of his life on the streets with owner James Bowen has been published and made into a film, *A Street Cat Named Bob*.

SHEPHERDESS WALK

78_THE SHERRIFF CENTRE

Hullabaloo – soft play in a church

Once upon a time, there was a Post Office that was due to close, so a local estate agent did a social media shoutout looking for suitable premises to keep this vital service running. Father Andrew, the then vicar of St James', offered the church as a fitting place for the relocation and it was decided that this would be a viable move. Planning commenced with The Sanctuary Café, and Hullabaloo soft play was later added into the mix. In 2014, with the church bells in full swing, The Sherriff Centre opened its doors.

The transformation is certainly a spectacle. Who'd have thought of having a Post Office, soft play, café and bar all under one roof? But it works, and the people love it. Where else can you fill in an application for a new passport with a chilled glass of wine, while the kids burn off some steam? The Sherriff Centre is also a charity offering free debt advice and The Food Share Project. So, buying a coffee while you visit not only gives you pleasure, it also helps support their great work.

Personally, the thought of heading to a soft play fills me with dread, but this isn't like any other soft plays. The church is stunning, with its high ceiling and large windows enabling light to flood through onto tall exposed brick arches. The juxtaposition with the primary colours of soft play adds fun for the kids. Make sure you keep an eye out for special events such as Hullabaloo Nights, where they fling open the doors after dark for a unique evening of late-night soft play with an open bar.

Address St James' Church, 2 Sherriff Road, London, NW6 2AP, +44 (0)207 625 1184, www.thesherriffcentre.co.uk // Getting there Tube to West Hampstead (Jubilee Line) // Hours Mon–Sat 9am–5pm // Ages 0+

TIP: Feeling creative? The pottery painting shop Art 4 Fun is just a five-minute walk from the Centre.

79_THE SILVER MOUSETRAP

Would you put a mousetrap on your head?

Established on Carey Street in 1690, this little shop has a very interesting tale. Currently the shop, A. Woodhouse & Son, is a family business that sells the most beautiful pieces of period jewellery, such as vintage bracelets, necklaces and earrings, as well as exceptional antique silver.

So why was it called The Silver Mousetrap for so long? Today, women might opt for a messy bun hairstyle – it's quick, easy and does the job, but back in the day rich women would spend a fortune having their hair turned into works of art. The taller and more extravagant, the better! The only problem with such extravagant hairdos was the need to keep them in place for weeks. You couldn't just wash and go. Having your hair *in situ* for weeks meant that naughty little mice would move into your luscious locks as you slept. What a public *faux pas* to be at an important social event, dressed in one's finest, only to have a little mickey scurry out of your barnet in front of fellow guests.

Ah ha! The Silver Mousetrap team had a genius idea. They created elegant mousetraps for these ladies to put around their head as they slept. A brilliant idea indeed, though you wouldn't want to be woken up in the night to the sound of a 'thwack' as the trap caught a little mouse right beside your face.

From the outside of the shop, you'll see a hanging sign that reads 'The Silver Mousetrap'. While extravagant wigs and the horrendous mouse problem may have diminished, I wonder if they still sell the infamous traps.

TIP: The Old Curiosity Shop on Portsmouth Street dates from the 16th century and is one of London's oldest shops. Famously, this shop is said to have inspired the book of its namesake by Charles Dickens.

The SILVER MOUSETRAP

Est. 1690

Address 56 Carey Street, London,
WC2A 2JB // Getting there Tube
to Chancery Lane (Central Line) //
Hours Shop frontage accessible
24 hours // Ages 8+

80_SOHO, SO NOSEY

Can you sniff out the seven hooters?

In 1997, during a rebellious move against the Big Brother society that we live in, with the ever-growing CCTV surrounding us, artist Rick Buckley decided to plant noses on walls around London. Taking moulds of his own nose, he *apparently* planted 35 of the casts and hid them in plain sight. The most famous pocket of noses is known as 'The Seven Noses of Soho'. At least five of them still remain in and around Soho, so can you find them?

Over the years, rumours have been born as to why the noses are there, which have nothing to do with Rick. One of the most famous being the nose on Admiralty Arch where legend has it that this nose is a tribute to the Duke of Wellington who was renowned for his huge schnoz! Since this nose is at waist height for somebody riding past on horseback, mounted soldiers would rub 'Wellington's nose' for good luck as they rode through the arch.

Take a jaunty walk along any of the streets below, where the noses may remain and see if you can find them. Be warned... it's 'snot' easy – some are harder to sniff out than others!

This super fun nose hunt will take you on a tour of Soho, Covent Garden and into Trafalgar Square. You can choose the order you wish to walk, but I recommend starting at Admiralty Arch (Trafalgar Square) then heading onto Great Windmill Street, Meard Street, Bateman Street, Dean Street, D'Arblay Street and finally Endell Street. Here you will finish up just around the corner from Floral Street, where you can check out more hidden treasures in the tip below.

Address Admiralty Arch, St James', London, SW1A 2WH // Getting there Train or tube to Charing Cross (Northern and Bakerloo Lines) or tube to Embankment (Northern, Bakerloo, District and Circle Lines) // Hours Accessible 24 hours // Ages 5+

TIP: Shhhh, even the walls have ears! Along Floral Street are two hidden ears. Artist Tim Fishlock took a cast of his own ears and hid them in two separate locations along Floral Street, Covent Garden.

81_ ST BRIDE'S CHURCH

Why is a wedding cake tiered?

If you, like me, have an enquiring mind, then one question you may have asked yourself is 'Why are wedding cakes tiered?'. Let's face it, wedding cakes aren't cheap, and so many people opt for fake tiers with just a couple of real cake tiers to feed their guests. So why is a tiered cake so sought after for so many couples' big day?

St Bride's Church is nestled away on St Bride's Avenue, just off Fleet Street. You could quite easily walk past the turning without noticing it, and most people do, as they are too busy staring at their phone screens nowadays. Enter St Bride's Avenue and you'll find this wonderful church in all its glory, especially when the sun hits its spire. And there you have it, the spire. Does it remind you of anything?

The church and the grounds you stand on have been around for 2,000 years. Venture downstairs into the crypt to see an extremely rare artefact – a Victorian iron casket dating from the days of the infamous body snatchers Burke and Hare (that's a story for another time) which deterred those who exhumed bodies to earn a pound. The church of course has seen many redevelopments over time, one key build being after the Great Fire of London in 1666, which took nine years. Sir Christopher Wren led the project and designed the steeple. But what came first, the steeple or the cake? Mr Rich, a local baker, took the Wren design and baked a glorious wedding cake. The design of this new wedding cake and its widespread popularity made Mr Rich, well, rich!

Address Fleet Street, London, EC4Y 8AU, +44 (0)207 427 0133, www.stbrides.com // Getting there Tube to Blackfriars (Circle and District Lines) // Hours Mon–Fri 8am–5pm, Sat 10am–3.30pm, Sun 10am–6.30pm // Ages 5+

TIP: Speaking of cake, why not pop into one of the many bakeries in the area for a slice of deliciousness?

82_ST KATHARINE DOCKS

Charles Dickens would approve

A hop, a skip and a jump away from Tower Bridge sits St Katharine Docks. Located at the east of Central London, the docks have a tie with Pimlico in the west. Thomas Cubitt was contracted to develop Pimlico, but the land was marshy and unsuitable to build on. Using reclaimed soil excavated during the construction of St Katharine Docks, incredible rows of white stucco terraces were built. Some of the largest and most opulent houses were built around St George's Square, all thanks to the soil from the docks.

Back east, there's plenty to do at the docks from simply admiring the boats, to dining, or attending one of their annual events, the classic boat festival being one of them. Over 40 vintage boats of all shapes, sizes and historical relevance, fill the basin for a day of boat-building workshops, live music, food and children's activities. The annual tea-dance is a fabulous day for all with music from the 1920s to the 1950s. All are welcome to have a dance, dress in costumes from the era and, of course, enjoy tea and biscuits. While there, you cannot help but admire The Dickens Inn with its welcoming floral balconies. It was opened in 1976 by the great-grandson of Charles Dickens, who stated 'My Great Grandfather would have loved this inn'.

Ping! 'I've got a text!'. OK, *Love Island* reference aside, did you know that in 1985 the first public mobile phone call was made right here in St Katharine Docks? The phone weighed 11 pounds – heavier than a newborn baby! How technology has developed over the years…

> TIP: Wizards gather, for you must attend the School of Magic to find the Golden Egg before the Dark Lord arrives at No1escape – an escape room suitable for kids aged 8+.

172

Address 50 St Katharine's Way, London, E1W 1LA, +44 (0)207 264 5312, www.skdocks.co.uk // Getting there Tube to Tower Hill (Circle and District Lines) // Hours Accessible 24 hours // Ages 0+

83_ ST MARTIN-IN-THE-FIELDS

Is all this brass rubbing off on you?

Towering over a corner of Trafalgar Square, St Martin-in-the-Fields is a glorious historical landmark and working church. The current design has been there since 1726, and over the years the church has supported the community immensely. One of its continuing programmes is in support of London's homeless people, helping around 7,500 a year.

Below the church you will find the crypt, a superb space of exposed brick ceilings and arches, and an old paved floor containing historic tombs. It's a wonderfully warming environment to sit and enjoy food from the café by day and music events by night.

What do you get if you cross brass, paper and wax crayons? Today, a child's Christmas wish list may be bursting with modern toys and fancy tech, but years ago children's entertainment was far less jazzy. One popular pastime in the Victorian era was brass rubbing. In the crypt, families can discover this art and take their rubbing home to keep. The church has a vast selection of brass rubbing to choose from, which are based on brasses from churches and cathedrals across the UK. Styles include William Shakespeare, knights in armour, fire-breathing dragons, religious scenes, lions and more. Simply pick a brass design, chat to the St Martin's team, who will help you choose your paper and wax crayons, and rub away until the brass image comes through on your paper.

It's a fun activity for all ages, plus, the café does a great sponge cake and custard reminiscent of school dinners (in a good way!).

Address The Crypt at St Martin-in-the-Fields, Trafalgar Square, London, WC2N 4JH // Getting there Train or tube to Charing Cross (Northern and Bakerloo Lines) or tube to Embankment (Northern, Bakerloo, District and Circle Lines) // Hours Daily 11am–5pm // Ages 5+

TIP: The National Gallery (just opposite here) has a host of family activities throughout the year.

84_ST PAUL'S CATHEDRAL

Shhhhhh

Prominent across the London skyline for hundreds of years, St Paul's Cathedral offers a rather quirky experience. Famous across the globe for its spectacular architecture, it has survived 57 consecutive nights of bombings during the Blitz, experienced a visit in 1964 from Martin Luther King, who delivered a sermon to 4,000 worshippers, and of course hosted the magnificent royal wedding between Prince Charles and Lady Diana Spencer in 1981. The cathedral is, and will always remain, an important place of worship that welcomes hundreds of congregations a year. Religious and non-religious visitors flock to the cathedral to explore its history and discover hidden wonders.

Shhhhhh…

Families can take part in activities, complete quizzes and play interactive games. Cathedral guides are also available in multiple languages, giving maximum inclusion to visitors. Throughout the year you can marvel at the art that fills the interior, and take your time exploring the Sir Christopher Wren exhibition to learn more about the architect who designed the cathedral as we see it today, over 300 years ago.

The imposing dome is one of the world's largest, standing 366 feet tall. It is open to visitors, and offers a superb 360-degree view of London. But that's not all. Head inside and stand anywhere along the wall of the dome. What can you hear? Probably the whispers of people opposite who are over 100 feet away! It's nicknamed 'the whispering dome', and I'd advise keeping your secrets to yourself, as you never know who is listening.

Address St Paul's Churchyard, London, EC4M 8AD, +44 (0)207 246 8350, www.stpauls.co.uk // Getting there Tube to St Paul's (Central Line) // Hours Mon, Tue, Thu, Fri & Sat from 8.30am, Wed from 10am // Ages 0+

85_STOKE NEWINGTON TOWN HALL

Really good camouflage is hard to find

A town hall is a town hall. You might not really give it a second thought. They are strewn across the country where local government officials and employees work. You can even get married in one if you so fancy. But there is one town hall that is unique among the collection. Stand back and look at Stoke Newington Town Hall. What can you see? Look closely.

Adorning the façade are large painted patches in different earthy shades. This is in fact camouflage. During the Blitz, in a ploy to hide the newly opened building from overhead bombing, the town hall was painted camo style to dim its fresh bright tone. A blackout was mandatory in London, meaning that all lights must be switched off in darkness, but even under the light of the moon this new build stood out, and therefore the decision was made for it to be painted so it was hidden from the enemies flying above. Strategically, this was an important move, as the basement of the town hall accommodated the Stoke Newington Civil Defence Control Centre. They even reinforced the ceilings to ensure additional safety for employees. The reinforcement and camouflage paint are still there today.

On the corner of Clissold Park, the camouflage will have helped the building blend in with the park. Be sure to take a look around the whole exterior of the building to get a true sense of the scale of this cover-up. While Stoke Newington took a big hit, the town hall suffered only minor damage. Could this have been down to its disguise?

TIP: Clissold House, deer and goat parks, and playground are just next door.

178

Address Church Street, London, N16 0JR // Getting there Overground to Stoke Newington // Hours Viewable from the outside only // Ages 5+

86_STREATHAM ICE AND LEISURE CENTRE

Get your skates on!

During the winter months, multiple outdoor ice rinks pop up in various London boroughs. Come January, they pack up and are put away for another year. There are, however, a few places where ice lovers can skate all year round.

Ice first came to Streatham in 1831. The beautiful Art Deco building stood proud for 80 years, with hundreds of budding ice skaters flooding through the doors of Silver Blades as it was known then. You can watch a great short film of archive footage set in the old ice rink during its heyday, on the British Film Institute's BFI Player website. When the building fell into disrepair it was demolished and rebuilt, re-opening in 2013 as Streatham Ice and Leisure Centre, a state-of-the-art sports complex with an Olympic-sized ice rink. Whether you are a seasoned pro, or a complete beginner, they cater for all levels.

If you are an ice hockey fan, Streatham Ice Hockey Club play home games here most weekends from September through to March and you are welcome to attend. To be one of the 900+ spectators, head to their website for fixtures and tickets.

TIP: Visit The Rookery, an Old English Garden of ornamental ponds and wildflower beds.

You may even see some celebrities from *Dancing On Ice* rehearsing on their own silver blades! How about being a celebrity in your own right? The leisure centre offers children's ice-skating birthday parties, so little ones can be the star of their own show and dance on the ice with their friends.

Address 390 Streatham High Road, London, SW16 6HX, +44 (0)208 677 5758, www.active.lambeth.gov.uk // Getting there Train to Streatham Common // Hours Mon–Fri 6am–10pm, Sat & Sun 7am–7pm // Ages 5+

87_SWISS GLOCKENSPIEL

A chime with charm

The Swiss Glockenspiel has been in Leicester Square for many years. Originally it was on the outside of the Swiss Centre. Opened in 1968, this 14-storey glass and steel Modernist tower was designed to showcase all Switzerland has to offer (which included a Swiss bank and, yes, chocolate of course) and drive tourism that way. The charming glockenspiel was so popular that London tour buses would stop outside on the hour to let tourists off the bus to see the masterpiece in action. They would then reboard the bus and carry on their journey.

In 2008 when the centre was demolished to make way for the W Hotel and M&M World, locals were sad to see the wonderful clock disappear. All hope was not lost, as the Swiss Glockenspiel was painstakingly restored by clockmakers Smith of Derby. It returned in 2011 just a few yards from its original location.

Now 33 feet up, high on a post at the Swiss Court entrance to Leicester Square, the clock once more proudly shows off its 27 bells and charming figurines in Swiss national costume. As the clock strikes the hour, the bells chime and the figures move around the clock to a merry tune. The music that tings out from the bells was written by London's Royal Academy of Music and the University for Music and Art in Berne.

Just beyond the clock you'll see a post displaying flags of all the cantons of Switzerland, which used to be on the Swiss Centre along with the clock. Can you name any of the cantons? A clue – there are 26 of them.

Address Swiss Court, London, W1D 6BY // Getting there Tube to Leicester Square (Piccadilly and Northern Lines) // Hours Accessible 24 hours // Ages 4+

TIP: There's a superhero in town! Leicester Square has a free interactive trail for you to search high and low for 10 famous characters including Batman, Bugs Bunny, Harry Potter and Paddington.

88_SYON HOUSE AND PARK

An exploding king

What do Pocahontas and one of the Gunpowder Plotters have in common? They both visited Syon. More specifically, Pocahontas lived here for six months, and Thomas Percy (the plotter), visited the day before the failed attempt to blow up parliament. Other well-known visitors to the Syon estate include Queen Victoria as a child taking her queen lessons, and the cast for TV productions such as *Downton Abbey* and *Bridgerton*.

Built in the early 16th century, Syon House came under the ownership of the Percy family in 1594 and is still in the family today. Many people have stayed over the years, and one particular overnight stay makes for a grim tale. After his death in 1547, Henry VIII's body lay in state at Whitehall Palace before being transported to Windsor Castle to be laid to rest. *En route*, in the days before motor vehicles, his cortège stopped at Syon House for the night to break up the long journey. Overnight, due to the rickety carriage ride shaking everything about, the body of the late monarch exploded! I wonder if the Percys knew this when taking over the estate 50 years later.

A visit today is far more pleasant. There is a wondrous Great Conservatory, with a magnificent dome, used to house exotic plants that grow right to the top. Just imagine the size of them. The gardens are great for exploring and there are trails to follow – you can play 'the floor is lava' on old tree stumps in one of the natural play areas and, finally, end the year with a spooky visit at Halloween and hear more tales.

Address Syon Park, Brentford, TW8 8JF, +44 (0)208 560 0882, www.syonpark.co.uk // Getting there Train to Syon Lane or Brentford, or tube to Boston Manor (Piccadilly Line) then E8 bus; Gunnersbury (District Line or Overground) then bus 237 or 267; Ealing Broadway (Elizabeth, District & Central Line) then bus E8 or E2 // Hours House: Wed, Thu & Sun 10.30am–4.30pm; gardens: Wed–Sun 10.30am–4.30pm (daily in school holidays) // Ages 0+

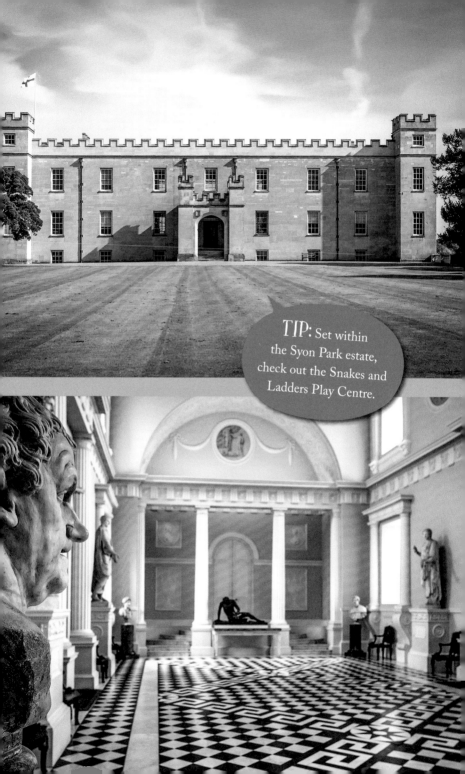

TIP: Set within the Syon Park estate, check out the Snakes and Ladders Play Centre.

89_TATE BRITAIN

Calling all mini artists

Along the north side of the River Thames at Mill-bank is one of the world's most renowned art galleries. Built on the grounds of an old reform prison, Tate Britain opened in 1897. Focusing on British art from the 16th century to the present day, it houses the world's largest collection of J. M. W. Turner's paintings.

It is also home to the Turner Prize (named after J. M. W. Turner of course!), an annual award that is given to an artist working in the UK, aged under 50, who has created an outstanding exhibition of work in the previous 12 months.

If you have your eyes on the prize, then Tate Britain nurtures the creativity of mini artists throughout the year. It hosts a series of free events, and families can enjoy workshops such as Story Space, 'a place for all to read, imagine, play and create'. They also have Tate Draw, where children can draw a picture and see their creation displayed on a digital screen for all to view. The Play Studio is also great fun. Children can dress up and place themselves in an artwork collection while exploring sound and vision in the studio.

When leaving the gallery, turn and look back. In the past, the exterior of the Tate has been transformed by mesmerising installations, a wonderful example being Chila Kumari Singh Burman's *Remembering a Brave New World*, which consisted of hundreds of multi-coloured neon lights covering the whole façade to coincide with Diwali. Look across the River Thames for a great view of the Secret Intelligence Service MI6 building.

TIP: In Victoria Tower Gardens you can enjoy the riverside playground and admire the Buxton Memorial Fountain, celebrating the abolition of slavery and commemorating the work of MP Thomas Fowell Buxton.

Address Millbank, London, SW1P 4RG,
+44 (0)207 887 8888, www.tate.org.uk //
Getting there Tube to Pimlico (Victoria
Line) // Hours Daily 10am–6pm // Ages 6+

90_TEDDINGTON LOCK AND WEIR

Seal of approval

Here marks the spot where the River Thames becomes non-tidal. Teddington has been around since the Anglo-Saxon age and has developed over time to be one of the most desirable places to live along the Thames. As the village expanded and the population grew, Teddington Lock and Weir was constructed to control the river. After originally being built with timber, and a few more rebuilds after that, the lock you see today was finished in 1904. The river was lively and the people of the bustling village needed a way to cross the water, so a ferry service was introduced. This was replaced in 1889 by the two foot bridges you can cross today.

The weir is a lovely spot to walk, cycle and swim. With steps leading down to the beach, on sunny days families head to the water to cool off; dogs love it too. You'll see little boats sailing in and out of the weir as well as people doing water sports along the river. If you are lucky, you may even spot a seal; there are information boards stating the dos and don'ts if you are fortunate enough to see one. Who knew seals lived in this part of the Thames? On one rare occasion, in 2021, a minke whale calf found its way into the weir. people flocked to the foot bridge to observe the lost sea creature before it was taken away by the rescue team.

> TIP: Set in an old church, the Landmark Arts Centre has plenty for families to do.

Ham Lands Local Nature Reserve is on the north side of the weir and features various ecological zones. It's a popular setting for families, nature lovers and horse riders. BMX fans can also dip into the off-road track.

Address Teddington Lock,
Teddington, TW11 9NG //
Getting there Train to Teddington //
Hours Accessible 24 hours // Ages 0+

91__THAMES BARRIER

London's flood defence

Since visiting on a school trip in the 1990s, I've had a real appreciation for the Thames Barrier. It is a wonderful example of protective engineering, being one of the largest movable steel flood barriers in the world. The sheer scale of each section is astounding. Reminiscent of the Sydney Opera House with its giant curved clad shell, the barrier uses primary yellow-coloured rocker beams that add to its distinctive look. Lined like a row of protective ships, it is divided into seven sections, each with a submerged gate that rises to control the flow of water.

Rising water levels caused by global warming have meant an increase in the need for such a barrier. Protecting London from high tides and storm surges is why this water beast of machinery was installed in 1984 over a 1,700-foot-wide stretch of the Thames between the boroughs of Greenwich to the south and Newham to the north. Traffic lights alert boats to when they can pass through. To see the barrier in action, they test it once a month for maintenance; times are listed on the website.

How likely is London to flood? The last two major floods were in 1928, when the water burst over embankments into Whitehall and Westminster. After this was the flood of 1953 caused by a storm surge from the North Sea. Subsequent discussions began regarding how to protect London.

TIP: Thames Barrier Park on the Newham side is a lovely green space with a playground.

The Thames Barrier is supported by other defences along the river with miles of walls and embankments, barriers and gates, and hundreds of outfalls and pumps.

Address 1 Unity Way, London, SE18 5NJ, www.gov.uk/guidance/the-thames-barrier // Getting there Train to Woolwich Dockyard // Hours Accessible 24 hours // Ages 4+

92_THAMES CYCLE PATH

Tripcock Ness to Crossness Incinerator

Cycling along the Thames Path is one of my absolute favourite things to do, and here's why. There is no traffic, and importantly, no hills – perfect! There are multiple cycle routes to choose from in London. Transport for London have some free online guided routes that you can choose from if you aren't sure. They also offer a free Cycle Skills school for adults and children at all skill levels. One particular course is Cycle Safely on Busy Roads and at Junctions – a really helpful session, especially for those cycling in London.

This chapter focuses on the Thames Path South Bank Section 4b of the Thames Pathway by Go Jauntly. It's a shared pathway for pedestrians and cyclists at the east end of the River Thames, and takes you from Tripcock Ness to Crossness Incinerator (approximately two and a half miles). Cycling along the South Bank is a great way to explore Central London and beyond, but it can get very busy with pedestrians in hot spots such as outside Tate Modern. Heading further east, the landscape changes and becomes more industrial, with a particular highlight being the view over to Barking Creek. You'll see two towers that operate the drop-gate flood barrier protecting the creek. Further along you'll reach Crossness Pumping Station.

There are plenty of places to stop along the way should you want to grab some water and take in the view. The route is also really well sign posted so you can easily pop to a shop or into the nearest railway station.

Address Margaret Ness Lighthouse, London, E6 7FF, www.walks.gojauntly.com/walks/thames-path-south-bank-section-4b-3361677336792404461 // Getting there Train to Plumstead // Hours Accessible 24 hours // Ages 0+

93_THAMES ROCKETS

Speed along the river like James Bond

Thames Rockets have zoomed into the number one spot as the best outdoor activity in London, and it's easy to see why. For the thrill seeker, it makes for a unique way to discover the River Thames. Starting at Waterloo, just beneath the London Eye, the red rocket awaits you. The Ultimate London Adventure tour (50 minutes) begins with a nice mosey along the river, set to curated music that adds to the experience. Once you pass under Tower Bridge, it's time to hold onto your hat!

The rocket engine lets loose and thrusts you along, bouncing on waves, twisting and turning along to up-tempo tunes past Canary Wharf. Just when you think it's over, the boat does a U-turn and repeats all the way back to Tower Bridge, returns to a slower pace, and the wonderful actor/comedian guide points out the famous sights with interesting facts. You'll see the Tower of London and catch a glimpse of Traitors' Gate, pass HMS *Belfast*, look up at the Walkie Talkie and the Shard, see the three Blackfriars bridges (yes three!), learn that the lion heads along the embankment wall aren't just there for decoration – they are in fact there for a very good reason – and finally potter past the Houses of Parliament and see where the MPs have a drink after work.

This experience is a must-do when in London. Don't let the weather put you off. If it rains, they offer you free ponchos (wear one or you'll be soaked!). They also offer lots of other experiences, including spooky Halloween rides, Santa rides and exclusive kids' parties.

Address Boarding Gate One, The London Eye Pier, London, SE1 7PB, +44 (0)208 038 7788, www.thamesrockets.com // Getting there Train or tube to Waterloo (Northern, Bakerloo, Jubilee and Waterloo & City Lines) // Hours Daily 10am–sunset // Ages 5+ (under 14s must be accompanied)

TIP: Book onto the Thames Rockets' New Year's Eve ride for one of the best views of the London Firework displays. The ride includes nibbles, and of course a glass of bubbles or two! Kids are welcome.

94_THE TIN TABERNACLE

A battleship party venue

This corrugated iron church in north-west London is a rare example of its kind. Corrugated iron was popular in the 19th century as it was light, making it easy to transport. Prefabricated buildings of this type were popular across the British Empire. Starting as St James' church, the building has had many uses over time. During World War II it was an ARP centre where locals could learn about air raid shelters, and collect their gas masks. It has also been used as a cinema, gallery and performance space. Most interesting is its interior redesign, thanks to two sailors who entered the building and decided it would be the perfect location for Sea Cadets. With this, the interior was turned into a replica battleship. The ship also has a chapel with its own story. It was the original set from the film *Becket* starring Richard Burton, and it is right here that his character died. The film won an Oscar in 1965; visiting this chapel may be the closest most of us will ever get to one!

To visit, there are a few options. Firstly, the building takes part in Open House, a fantastic annual festival celebrating London's unique and vast architecture style. You can gain access to buildings across the city that are not usually open to the public. Another way to visit is to attend one of the events held in the building. Finally, you can hire the space… if you need a battleship party venue.

Humans aren't the only visitors. There is a cat that you might notice wandering about, presumably to keep mice at bay.

Address 12–16 Cambridge Avenue, North Maida Vale, London, NW6 5BA, www.tintabernaclekilburn.org // Getting there Tube to Kilburn Park (Bakerloo Line); train to Kilburn High Road // Hours Open days held every other Sat noon–3pm; check website for other events // Ages 6+

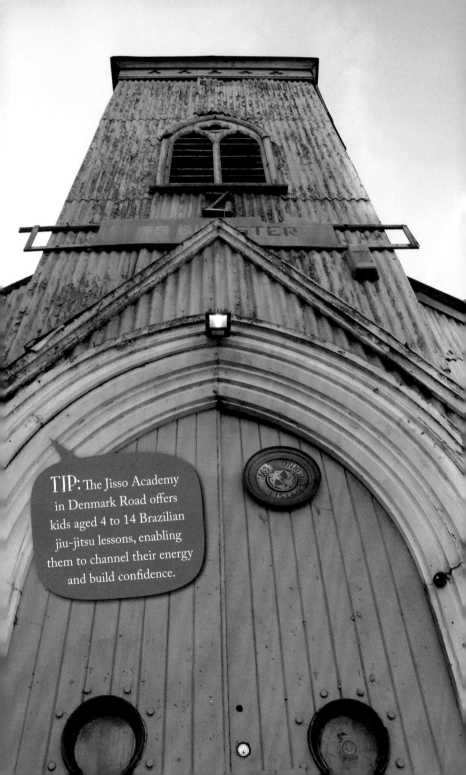

TIP: The Jisso Academy in Denmark Road offers kids aged 4 to 14 Brazilian jiu-jitsu lessons, enabling them to channel their energy and build confidence.

95_TOBACCO DOCK

A 1980s retail disaster

Wapping sits along the River Thames and was once a hub for shipping imports. The river spills into many basins, canals and marinas sprawled across the north side of the water. Along one of these pockets of water sits the Tobacco Dock. I first discovered it many years ago when I attended an event for industry darlings, and was amazed at how stunning the venue is. With exposed brickwork vaults, timber beams and a large open area with a huge glassed roof, it's easy to see why this has become a favourite spot for hosting events.

The Tobacco Dock takes its name from its highest imported product: tobacco from Virginia. It also housed items such as brandy, wool and molasses. At one time it was even visited by a tiger who had escaped from a nearby animal emporium. The tiger came across a young boy, grabbed him by his jacket and padded off to the Tobacco Dock. Luckily the boy was rescued by the emporium's owner. In the Pennington Street entrance is a statue of the boy and tiger.

Outside you'll find two replica pirate ships that were installed in the 1980s when the old warehouse was transformed into a shopping centre in the hope it would become the 'Covent Garden of the East End'. But it wasn't to be, and within a year of opening the shopping centre closed, leaving this enormous building derelict and unloved for years. Now, it makes for a nice family visit. While the inside is no longer open to the public for general visits, they do have events you can attend throughout the year.

TIP: Pelican Stairs, just to the right of the Prospect of Whitby, take you down onto Wapping Beach. There you'll also find a real noose where pirates were dangled from.

Address 50 Porters Walk, London, E1W 2SF, +44 (0)207 680 4001, www.tobaccodocklondon.com // Getting there Tube to Shadwell (East London Line); Overground to Wapping // Hours Accessible from the outside 24 hours a day; check website for special events // Ages 4+

96_TOOTING BEC LIDO

Jump in for a good time

If you fancy a fresh dip on a hot day, Tooting Bec Lido is a great spot to cool off. Perfect for a quick lunchtime swim or a longer visit with the kids, you'll have a fab time at the UK's oldest open-air swimming pool. Opening in 1906, Tooting Bathing Lake as it was then known was an immediate hit with locals. Back then, few homes had their own bathrooms, so the lido doubled up as a communal bath. Thankfully this isn't the case today!

Reopening in May 2024 after a £4,000,000 renovation, at 300 feet long there's plenty of room for everyone. The lido also includes a paddling pool for your little swimmers to splash about in, and the whole site is fully accessible, including a pool hoist. The colourful changing room doors give a hint to beach huts along the UK coast, and the onsite café offers a range of hot and cold refreshments; as the pool is open all year round, you may well need a hot chocolate after a chilly dip. Yep, chilly. The pool is unheated, so take care if you want to surround yourself with a million gallons of unheated water!

The South London Swimming Club has been based at the lido since the very start. The club offers both open events and members' events, which include Summer Synchro for anyone aged 10+ to learn how to synchronise swim, and the Rookie Lifeguard class for those aged 8–14 years to learn confidence and safety in the water.

You don't have to be a member to access the pool, as you can buy session passes (under fives go free). There's also a picnic area, so pack your sarnies!

Address Tooting Bec Road, London, SW16 1RU, +44 (0)144 422 1052, www.placesleisure.org/centres/tooting-bec-lido // Getting there Train to Streatham or tube to Tooting Bec (Northern Line) // Hours Open access Apr–Sept but hours vary daily, so check website; 365-day access for South London Swimming Club members // Ages 0+

TIP: Bertie and Boo Adventure Island is a wonderful, imaginative family play centre and café.

97_TOWER BRIDGE

A glass platform over the Thames

Tower Bridge is one of London's most photographed bridges. You may have walked over it, but did you know you can go inside? In 1886 construction began, but without today's strict health and safety regulations, and so workmen would be scaling the site at significant height completely unsecured. You'll feel queasy just looking at the old construction photos. Let's not forget the divers who went deep down to the river bed to work on the foundations, which are 26 feet deep.

Visiting Tower Bridge takes you into the heart of the history and current operations of the bridge. The Engine Room houses one of the original steam-powered engines that would be used to lift the bridge daily, allowing boats to pass through. When the use of electricity came along in 1976, the engines were retired, but one has been kept onsite for visitors to view up close. You can see the bridge lift on various days and times as listed on the website. In fact, the bridge must give priority to travellers on the water, so at any point the bridge can open to let a ship pass, which can be frustrating if you are on the road and in a rush to get to the other side.

High above the water (137 feet in fact) you can cross the walkway, if you dare! Some of the floor panels are made of glass, giving a unique view of the river, pedestrians and vehicles below. Fret not: apparently the glass is strong enough to hold the weight of two black taxis, which is the weight I often feel after a Sunday roast dinner! Perhaps I'll visit on a Tuesday...

TIP: Off with their heads! To see where Anne Boleyn lost her noggin, the Beefeaters and their ravens, and the Crown Jewels, head (ahem) to the Tower of London just next door.

Address Tower Bridge Road, London,
SE1 2UP, +44 (0)207 403 3761,
www.towerbridge.org.uk // Getting there
Tube to Tower Hill (Circle and District Lines) //
Hours Daily 9.30am–6pm // Ages 4+

98_TREASURE TRAILS

Calling all secret agents!

Exploring a new area can be daunting, as you don't always know which way to turn. Treasure Trails are a fantastic way to discover a new area while having fun and learning along the way, plus you don't have to think about where you are heading as it's all written out for you with simple, easy-to-follow directions.

When my daughter was born, I'd take her in the pram and along with her dad we would choose a Treasure Trail to follow, whether it was in London or further afield, such as the Lake District, Manchester, Cornwall or the Isle of Wight. Oblivious as a baby, through the years she has begun to get involved and help us look for clues and follow directions. This chapter focuses on the Kingston upon Thames trail, but there is a wonderful selection of trails to choose from across the London boroughs. Many areas the trails cover are listed in this book, so you really could make a day of exploration.

Kingston is a lovely town set on the edge of the River Thames, with some great riverside dining options. The trail takes you on a self-guided spy mission walking trail of discovery through the old marketplace and along the river. Each clue takes you a step closer to cracking the code! If you get stuck, they offer a text message service with clues, which thankfully we've never had to use. Trails are available instantly via a download (you can print at home if needed), or you can opt to have one posted to you.

Always read the next direction to ensure you haven't walked too far and missed a vital clue!

TIP: Check out David Mach's sculpture *Out of Order*, which shows a row of red telephone boxes tumbled like dominos.

Address Market House, Kingston upon Thames, KT1 1JS, +44 (0)1872 263692, www.treasuretrails.co.uk // **Getting there** Train to Kingston // **Hours** Accessible 24 hours // **Ages** 0+

99_TRINITY BUOY WHARF

A lighthouse in London

A wonderfully chilled wharf on the Thames filled with colour, history and art at every turn, Trinity Buoy Wharf emanates playfulness and learning through its collection of sculptures and educational hubs. It's home to London's only remaining experimental lighthouse, constructed in 1864 to test and improve lighting, and used for the training of lighthouse workers. On certain days you can go inside and up to the top of the lighthouse. It's also home to the Longplayer, a 1,000-year-long musical composition made by Tibetan singing bowls that began on 31 December, 1999, and will continue to play unrepeated with the help of computer generation until the last moment of 2999 – let's hope the neighbours don't mind!

Trinity Buoy Wharf is also where you'll find The Faraday Effect, one of London's smallest museums, an immersive recreation of Michael Faraday's workshop filled with old photos, quirky objects, handwritten notes and one object that my daughter described as 'a dead cat'. It's actually a sleeping cat relaxing in a basket, though I didn't get close enough to check if it was a stuffed toy or a taxidermy feline. This is a fascinating space in what is essentially a small shed facing the river. Sit in Faraday's chair and look out through the open door across the water.

There is a café at the wharf, so you can buy food and drinks. You could also take a picnic and sit on one of the benches overlooking the river towards the O$_2$ Centre. See if you can spot the cable cars travelling over the Thames to the east.

Address 64 Orchard Place, London, E14 0JW, +44 (0)207 515 7153, www.trinitybuoywharf.com // Getting there Tube to Canning Town (Jubilee Line); DLR to East India Station // Hours Daily 7am–7pm (excluding Christmas Day) // Ages 0+

TIP: Bow Creek & East India Dock Basin are both wildlife havens that give children a real insight into nature.

100_ TWO TEMPLE PLACE

Commissioned by one of the world's richest men

Temple is a fantastic area to explore, especially at the weekend, as it's pretty much deserted. Every barrister in England and Wales must, to this day, belong to one of the four legal societies – the 'Inns of Court', which are located here. As you meander through two of these Inns, Inner Temple and Middle Temple, you'll notice names on boards at building entrances. These are the names of the tenant barristers practising from the chambers in those buildings.

In the centre of the Temple area, in Fountain Court, you'll find a tranquil space with a fountain that has been at its heart for over 300 years. Once built, the water fountain was thought to be the first permanent structure of its kind in London.

South of here, along the Embankment, is Two Temple Place, a splendid Neo-Gothic building commissioned in 1892 by one of the world's richest men, William Waldorf Astor. Today, you can step inside this wondrous Victorian building and see that no expense was spared. The interior is adorned with intricate carved oak panels, exquisite mahogany figures from stories, books and plays, and great ebony columns. Now banned, the use of ebony back then was only for the rich and used as a status symbol. The magnificence of the stained-glass windows is worthy of its own trip. Families are welcome to visit for The House of Stories, interactive trails and creative workshops. Temple area as a whole is a hidden gem that is well worth exploring, away from the multitude of tourists in Central London.

Address 2 Temple Place, Temple, London, WC2R 3BD, +44 (0)207 836 3715, www.twotempleplace.org // Getting there Tube to Temple (Circle and District Lines) // Hours Open Jan–Apr and on select days throughout the year (check website) // Ages 6+

TIP: Check out the supervised hawks at Lincoln's Inn, one of the four Inns, which are used to deter seagulls from stealing barristers' wigs!

101_VALENTINES MANSION

Blooming roses

Experience life as a Victorian in this splendid house. Originally built in 1696, the building has had many uses over the years. In the 20th century it housed wartime refugees, was transformed into a hospital and, in more recent years, was used for the council housing department. Today, it has been recreated to its original state with a large Victorian kitchen and Georgian bedchamber. On arrival you'll receive a free visitor guide that highlights areas of interest, and if you're a bit more techie, try the new audio guide using a smart device to scan codes and listen to a brief history as you explore the house.

For families, the sounds and shadows trail is great fun for all! Listen out for voices from the past as you enter the rooms and look out for special shadows on the walls. The exciting events calendar includes children's activities during school holidays. Exhibitions come in all forms, a highlight being the 2024 photography showcase of East London images captured by super talented local Muslim women. Outside is just as special. Grab a bite to eat from The Gardener's Cottage Café then wander through the walled garden to the canal where you will see ducks and geese relaxing on the water's edge, and in spring you'll see swans with their cygnets. You'll also find a grotto. The rose garden blooms in summer and smells divine. There is also a children's play area on the side of the park, just a short walk or scoot away! With all of this, it's easy to see why Valentines is an award-winning park.

Address Emerson Road, Ilford, IG1 4XA, +44 (0)208 708 8100, www.valentinesmansion.com // Getting there Train or tube to Ilford (Elizabeth Line), or Gants Hill (Central Line) // Hours Sun & Mon Mar–Oct noon–5pm, Nov–Feb 11am–3pm // Ages 0+

TIP: Little Free Library on Brisbane Road is a cute cupboard library where you can freely take or leave a book. There are many of these dotted all over London – just check out the LFL map online.

102_ VAUXHALL CITY FARM

A hidden gem in the shadow of MI6

Where do MI6 spies have lunch? Well, I can't tell you that as it's top secret! But they *might* pop over the road to The Old Dairy café at Vauxhall City Farm.

This farm, close by the River Thames, is home to over 100 animals, a café and dozens of annual education and youth projects. Before this, in 1976, the land was used by a group of architects who were squatting. In a collaborative move with local residents, they began growing vegetables and caring for livestock. Since then, the farm has grown to become a staple part of the community, which brings inner city people together to experience a taste of farm life.

On arrival, grab a bag or two of animal feed and follow the pathway into the farm to feed the alpacas, goats and sheep. Bonnie and Clyde will also be waiting for you – the farm's pigs, not the notorious bank robbers! Hop along further to see the rabbits, chickens, turkeys and an aviary full of our feathered friends. The farm also offers meet and greets with the animals so you can pet the floofs. Take a walk around their community garden – a lovely tranquil space full of seasonal plants and produce. In the café, you can try their hot soup, sandwiches and fresh pastries. In the evening, the café is transformed into Faith's Place bar where you can sample drinks from local breweries.

TIP: Bonnington Square Pleasure Garden is a tranquil play space for the kids and a haven of peace for adults, filled with both English and exotic plants.

Throughout the year, the farm hosts a wonderful line-up of events, which ramp up during the school holidays. You can even meet Father Christmas himself in their fantastic grotto in December.

Address 165 Tyers Street, London, SE11 5HS, +44 (0)207 582 4204, www.vauxhallcityfarm.org // **Getting there** Train or tube to Vauxhall (Victoria Line) // **Hours** Farm Tue–Sun 10.30am–4pm, although closing hours vary depending on events and bar opening times // **Ages** 0+

103_THE VIKTOR WYND MUSEUM

Fun and freaky

Just a stone's throw from Regent's Canal you will find the weird and wonderful Viktor Wynd Museum of Curiosities, Fine Art & Natural History. This is a museum like no other. If you want to see neat displays, informative captions and censorship then don't bother visiting. The beauty of this museum is its eclectic chaos. Simply put, no sooner have you spotted, admired and in some cases had a slight stomach turn at a ghastly item, your periphery will spot something else that will make you chuckle. Over and over. It's quirky, fun, naughty and charming all at the same time. This isn't an airy-fairy visit, so make sure your kids are up for a unique journey of discovery. They will need to be comfortable with grisly items such as dead animals and human skulls. Together, see if you can spot any or all of these curious items: an eerie mermaid (think Disney's Ariel but grey, scaly and mummified), unicorns from the deep sea, part of David Bowie's mullet, fairies, a giant leg bone (belonging to what?), a blue parrot, a boat made of matchsticks, and doodled toilet rolls.

While the museum is small, it has enough items to keep you busy for a while. Enter with an open mind and vibrant imagination, and be prepared for lots of questions from the kids! Entry to the museum is via a spiral staircase. Children are permitted in the venue until 5pm, so before you leave, treat them to a mocktail in the bar area, which also has interesting items on display. You can even sit with a taxidermy lion.

Address 11 Mare Street, Cambridge Heath Road, London, E8 4RP, +44 (0)208 533 5297, www.thelasttuesdaysociety.org // Getting there Overground to Cambridge Heath // Hours Tue–Fri 3–11pm, Sat noon–11pm, Sun noon–10pm // Ages 6+

TIP: Walk along the canal to Broadway Market for a spot of shopping and a wide selection of food.

104_ WALTHAMSTOW PUMPHOUSE MUSEUM

Dining in a tube carriage

This East London museum set in the original Grade II-listed pump house is a great place for kids (and adults) who have an interest in engineering. In fact, its primary goal is to get everyone interested in engineering, and they are doing a great job. At the heart of the pumphouse are two original Victorian steam engines used as part of the Walthamstow sewage network. You can see them in action at select times.

Another highlight is the two 1967 stock Victoria Line tube carriages, one of which has been restored so you can hop on board. Those of us who are old enough will notice the old moquette fabric, seating booths and dangling strap hangers to clutch onto as the train moved along. During selected evenings the tube carriage transforms into the 'Supper Club Tube' where diners aged 14+ can enjoy a six-course meal. Opt for a booth seat if you can!

Step into the train room to discover a fantastic model of the Weaver Line, from Liverpool Street to Chingford. Created by volunteers, this model is superb! There's a replica of the high street with cinema and shops as well as Walthamstow Marshes, and running trains whizzing around the track. They also offer free arts and crafts in the pumping room. Hungry? Nip to the café, or bring your own snacks to enjoy on the picnic bench. Make sure you pop over to see Dennis, one of only two remaining fire engines of this kind.

TIP: Walthamstow Toy Library is a greener way to play. You can rent toys and return them when your child is done. Simply swap for a 'new' toy for them to play with, thus saving yourself a fortune.

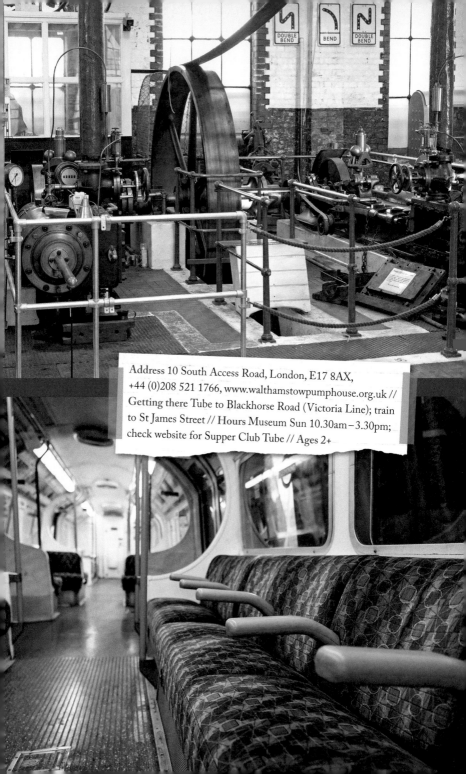

Address 10 South Access Road, London, E17 8AX,
+44 (0)208 521 1766, www.walthamstowpumphouse.org.uk //
Getting there Tube to Blackhorse Road (Victoria Line); train
to St James Street // Hours Museum Sun 10.30am – 3.30pm;
check website for Supper Club Tube // Ages 2+

105_WALTHAMSTOW WETLANDS

London Wildlife Trust

Just a few stops along the Victoria Line lies Walthamstow Wetlands, a beautiful nature reserve and reservoir. Free to enter, the Wetlands make for a great way to reconnect with nature away from the hustle and bustle of city life. Families can experience nature trails, pond dipping, guided walks, wildlife drawing, crafts and story-time sessions. Take your binoculars and look out for a variety of flourishing species that bring the landscape to life, such as the grey heron, kingfisher, tufted duck, rainbow trout, damselflies and even bats.

How many square yards are there in a hectare? Set over 160 hectares (that's a lot of square yards!) is the Thames Water reservoir. When you next pour a glass of water from the tap, or have a shower, think of this reservoir; it's the main source of water supply for approximately three and a half million people. If you are a fishing fan, then welcome to London's largest fishery. Permit-holding angling enthusiasts can fish in clear waters for carp, barbel, chub and bream. Two dedicated reservoirs also allow for fly fishing, with both brown trout and rainbow trout swimming below the surface.

Head along the water banks lined with shrubbery and look at views towards the inner city. It's a marvel to think how close this haven is to the concrete jungle. What's most charming is the seasonal change in the landscape. Before you leave, enjoy a hot drink or bite to eat inside the Engine House Visitor Centre or outside on the terrace, which offers stunning views over the reserve.

TIP: When in the East End, you have to try pie, mash and liquor. Barney's Pie & Mash will not be a wasted trip!

WILD FLOWER MEADOW

Address 2 Forest Road, Walthamstow, London, N17 9NH, +44 (0)203 989 7448, www.wildlondon.org.uk // Getting there Tube (Victoria Line) or train to Tottenham Hale // Hours Oct–Mar daily 9.30am–4pm, Apr–Sept 9.30am–5pm // Ages 0+

106_WELLINGTON ARCH

Take a peep into the king's back garden

Walking between Green Park and Hyde Park you venture through a traffic island and beneath a large arch. This is Wellington Arch. Originally this arch, along with Marble Arch, was built as a grand outer entrance to Buckingham Palace, but it wasn't to be and so Wellington Arch was later moved to its current location.

Wellington Arch became a victory arch declaring Wellington's defeat of Napoleon. Look up and you'll see a large bronze sculpture of a winged Angel of Peace landing behind a chariot of war being pulled by four horses that are led by a young boy at the reigns. Prior to this, there was a controversial statue of the Duke of Wellington on top of the arch, but this was later removed from its Central London spot and now sits near the Garrison Church at Aldershot.

In the 19th century, the inside of the arch was used by the parkkeeper and the police. Moving into the 20th century it once housed what was apparently London's smallest police station. So, if you were caught up to no good, you'd be brought here first.

The arch is now run by English Heritage and is open to the public. Inside you'll find a gift shop, exhibits showing the history of the arch, and viewing balconies. From the right angle you can peer into the garden of Buckingham Palace (better in the winter when there are fewer leaves on the trees!) and if you have timed your visit right, you'll see the Household Cavalry passing through on their way to and from the Changing of the Guard – a truly unique way to watch them.

Address Apsley Way, London, W1J 7JZ // Getting there Tube to Hyde Park Corner (Piccadilly Line) // Hours Exterior accessible 24 hours, interior Wed–Sun 10am–4pm // Ages 5+

TIP: For boutique shops and eateries head to Shepherd Market in Mayfair, the most expensive stop on the Monopoly board.

107_THE WHITE SWAN

Wading for a drink

Twickenham: the home of rugby, and a family-friendly pub with a beach! Set on the bank of the River Thames, The White Swan has been here since the 17th century and is apparently the oldest surviving pub in Twickenham. It has everything you need from a great pub; a cosy fireplace for those chilly winter evenings, a terraced balcony for when the sun is shining, delicious food with a kids' menu to boot, and of course a delightful drink selection. What makes this pub unique is that you can swim, row or paddle right up to it, as just out front is a small sandy beach loved by all.

That's at low tide. At high tide, the garden can become submerged as the river swells over the bank. It's fine though – just wear your wellies and pull up a pew, as the staff are well equipped to serve you at your table while your feet rest in the water. Those who aren't in the know when it comes to high tide, will find themselves sitting on the table top so as not to ruin their shoes. We were those unaware ones once when visiting with my daughter, who found it hilarious as we sat on our 'table boat' and daddy waded through the river to keep us fed and watered.

TIP: The Rolling Stones, The Who and Pink Floyd all performed on Eel Pie Island, accessible by the footbridge close by.

Keep an eye out for the multitude of activities occurring on the water. You'll see canoes and paddle boards that on occasion pull up on the beach, and if you're lucky you'll see the London Fire Brigade on a training exercise. In among all this you'll see ducks moseying along. I can honestly say it's one of my favourite, and more memorable, beer gardens in London.

Address Riverside, Twickenham, TW1 3DN, +44 (0)208 744 2951, www.whiteswantwickenham.co.uk // Getting there Train to Twickenham // Hours Sun–Tue 11am–10pm, Wed–Sat 11am–11pm // Ages 0+

108_ WINN'S COMMON PLAYGROUND

Power to the mums

Named after Thomas Winn, a landowner who built houses for destitute widows on what was then called Plumstead Common, Winn's Common has been a staple plot of green land enjoyed by hundreds of families for decades. An Act passed in 1878 ensured that at least 100 acres of green open space remains here in perpetuity.

Over time, the much-loved playground became lacklustre, and while kids with their playfulness and imagination would continue to enjoy it, the adults could see it needed a facelift. In 2019, two mums led an application for their local playground to be redeveloped. With the backing of Friends of Plumstead Common, they were awarded £60,000 from the Good Growth Fund to transform the space, an amazing achievement that came out of visualising the potential of the play area. The jazzed-up playground now includes staple playground items such as a slide, climbing ropes and swings, but the show stopper addition is a large pirate ship. This, along with disability inclusive equipment, has seen a new generation of families flood to the park come rain or shine to enjoy its modern offerings. To put their own stamp on it, Friends of Plumstead Common invited locals to paint the play area walls and the park keeper's building.

During the summer, the large paddling pool is cleaned and filled, adding another super soaker activity to your day out. On early maps, this padding pool and playground area was originally a boating lake. So, it's a nice circle back to its beginnings to have a large pirate ship installed.

Address Winn Common Road, London, SE18 1PH, +44 (0)208 856 0100, www.royalgreenwich.gov.uk // Getting there Train to Plumstead // Hours Playground: Sat & Sun 8am–8pm, Mon–Fri 6am–10pm; pool: 10am–6pm in summer // Ages 0+

TIP: Built up an appetite after all that fun? Using locally sourced suppliers, Plumstead Pantry offers a varied menu, with all food cooked to order by chef Jamie.

109_WOOLWICH FERRY

Forget Staten Island, we've got Woolwich

The Woolwich Ferry does what it says on the tin. Every day it ferries people, cars, bicycles and lorries from the north side of the River Thames to the south side, and back again. Ferrying along this route dates back to the 1300s when Woolwich was a fishing village. While there is no evidence that the service has been in action since then, it's apparent that the first services did take place then.

Fast forward to the late 1880s and the first free ferry crossing was established using paddle steamers. On its opening weekend in 1889, 25,000 people took rides across the Thames and back. The atmosphere was jubilant with flags and bunting, and excitement all around at this new crossing to the east of London. In 1963, motor ships were introduced, which could carry up to 500 passengers wanting to cross over to the other side. Today, the journey across the water takes no more than 10 minutes, and while onboard you can look west for a glimpse of the O_2 Centre, the Shard, Canary Wharf and the Thames Barrier. There are no facilities onboard, but as a foot passenger, you should be fine. If on the other hand you are in a vehicle, pack some snacks, as there can often be a queue to board, especially at rush hour. Oh, and did I mention it's free? What a bonus.

Also free to use is the Woolwich Foot Tunnel, just near the ferry entrance. Much like the Greenwich Foot Tunnel, a lift takes you down to the start of an underwater tunnel. Personally, I'd take the ferry for a quicker, more scenic ride.

TIP: Clockhouse Community Centre, set in a Grade II-listed building overlooking the river, has a lovely café, as well as events and family activities throughout the year.

Address New Ferry Approach, London, SE18 6DX, www.tfl.gov.uk/river-bus/timetable/woolwich-ferry // Getting there Train or tube to Woolwich (Elizabeth Line) // Hours See website for timetable // Ages 0+

110_ WORLD TIME LINEAR CLOCK

Pick a country and see what time it is!

You could easily walk past the World Time Linear Clock in Piccadilly Station without realising, and you'd certainly be missing a historical gem. Before its current layout, Piccadilly Circus Station's entrances were on the corner of Piccadilly and Haymarket with entrances on both streets. Where the Hard Rock Café now stands, you'd enter and descend into the tube.

By 1922, passenger numbers had grown to an incredible 18 million a year, and continued rising. To ensure the smooth flow of passengers into and out of the station, it was completely redeveloped, and in 1928 the station you see today opened.

As you meander through the crowds in the oval ticket hall (you'll soon see where the phrase 'it's like Piccadilly Circus' comes from!) keep an eye out for the World Time Linear Clock. It's a simple but skilful design: the central strip moves across a map of the world at the same speed as the Earth's rotation. Genius. You have to know your roman numerals to tell the time though! If you put your ear close to the clock, you can even hear it ticking away. You'll also see small lightbulbs that highlight particular cities. These cities acted as a reference point for those wanting to know the time around the world.

Leave the station via Exit 2, and once on street level you'll see one of the few surviving old blue police call posts, an important means of communication for the police force before they had personal radios. The call posts could also be used by the public to contact the police.

Address Piccadilly Circus, London, W1J 9HP // Getting there
Tube to Piccadilly Circus (Bakerloo and Piccadilly Lines) //
Hours Daily 8am–10pm // Ages 5+

TIP: Waterstones Piccadilly is Europe's largest bookshop. Head to the rooftop café for refreshments and a good read.

111_ YE OLDE SWISS COTTAGE

Alpine vibes on a traffic island

Can you guess which London Underground station is named after a pub? The clue is in this chapter's title. It is of course Swiss Cottage, situated on a traffic island along Finchley Road. As a child I used to venture past this pub on my way to the Odeon and always wondered what it was like inside, the exterior was so intriguing. Not to give any spoilers, but it is essentially a standard British pub interior with lovely little nods to Swiss style with hand-painted designs on the walls and furniture. However, it's the exterior that is of most interest.

Back in 1840, this coaching inn, then known simply as Swiss Tavern, was built. The landscape at the time would be unrecognisable today. Fields covered the land and it was here that working men travelling in and out of London stopped for a rest and the all-important traditional English bitter. The inn also housed a dairy selling milk and cheese. Over time, the green and pleasant land has developed into a grey urban part of London which, along with the tube station, took its name from the old inn. Even the pub, which was once sandy yellow in colour, has been repainted grey, but pops of colour remain on the shutters and columns.

With its Grade II-listed status, this pub isn't going anywhere. If you can't make it to the Alps this year, then sitting outside of this north London pub with a bite to eat on a sunny day is the next best thing… if you ignore the red buses regularly passing by that is. They also have Alpine lager on tap to add to the experience.

TIP: Primrose Hill offers uninterrupted views over London. What famous landmarks can you see from up there?

Address 98 Finchley Road, London, NW3 5EL, +44 (0)207 722 3487 // Getting there Tube to Swiss Cottage (Jubilee Line) // Hours Mon–Sat noon–11pm, Sun noon–10.30pm // Ages 0+

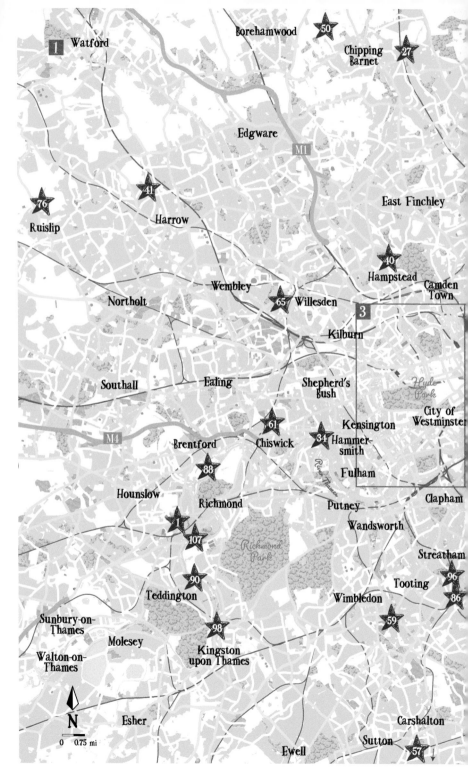

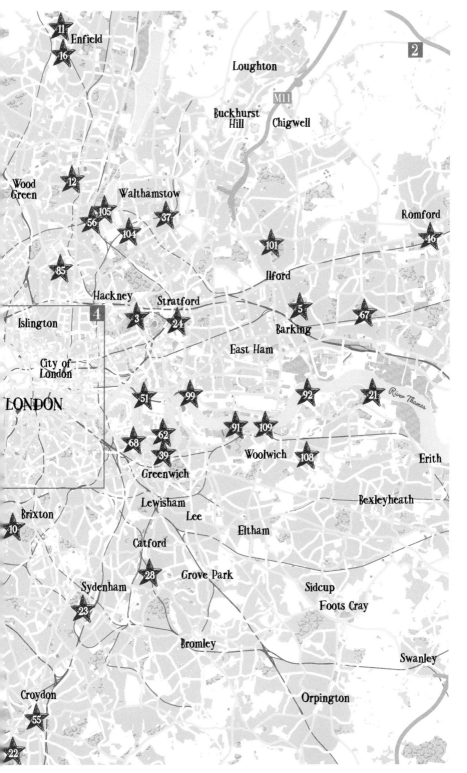

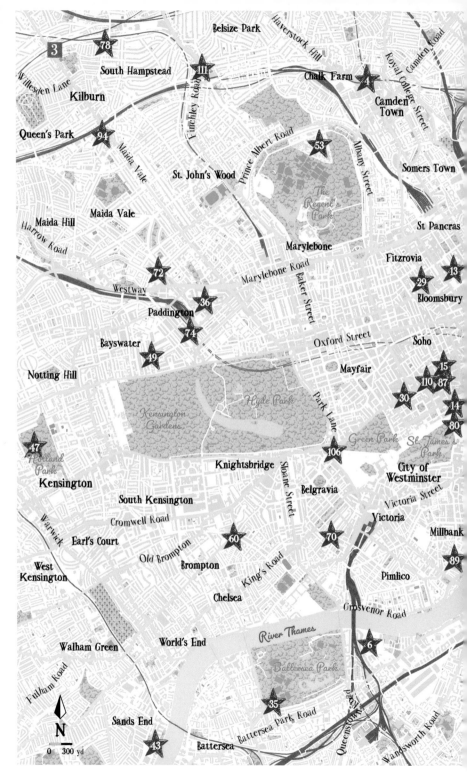

4

Highbury

Balls Pond Road

Graham Road

Hackney

Caledonian Road

York Way

Upper Street

Essex Road

Canonbury

Kingsland Road

Dalston

West Street

Victoria Park

Barnsbury

Islington

Haggerston

19

Pentonville Road

44

Hoxton

77

City Road

Goswell Road

Shoreditch

Hackney Road

Bethnal Green

103

7

King's Cross

31

71

Clerkenwell

Clerken Old Street

Finsbury

Whitechapel

Stepney

2

Holborn

High Holborn

City of London

64

42 79 25

73   81

84

75

Whitechapel

9 Covent
58   Garden
52   100

69

Shadwell

83

LONDON

54

32

18

82

Wapping

95

Rotherhithe Tunnel

93

38 17

66

20

Tooley Street

97

River Thames

48

Waterloo

63

The
Borough

Long Lane

Tower Bridge

Bermondsey

Lower Road

Southwark Park

Blackfriars Road

Southwark Bridge Road

33 Lambeth

Elephant and Castle

26

Walworth

Old Kent Road

Old Kent Road

Rotherhithe New

Vauxhall

Kennington

102

Walworth Road

Oval

8

Burgess Park

Clapham Road

Brixton Road

Camberwell

Peckham Road

Peckham

45

New Cross
Gate

Loughborough Junction

Martin Booth, Barbara Evripidou
111 Places for Kids in Bristol
That You Shouldn't Miss
ISBN 978-3-7408-1665-0

Evan Levy, Rachel Mazor,
Joost Heijmenberg
111 Places for Kids in New York
That You Must Not Miss
ISBN 978-3-7408-1993-4

John Sykes, Birgit Weber
111 Places in London
That You Shouldn't Miss
ISBN 978-3-7408-2379-5

Michael Glover, Benedict Flett
111 Hidden
Art Treasures in London
That You Shouldn't Miss
ISBN 978-3-7408-1576-9

Terry Philpot, Karin Tearle
111 Literary Places in London
That You Shouldn't Miss
ISBN 978-3-7408-1954-5

Emma Rose Barber,
Benedict Flett
111 Churches in London
That You Shouldn't Miss
ISBN 978-3-7408-0901-0

Solange Berchemin,
Martin Dunford, Karin Tearle
111 Places in Greenwich
That You Shouldn't Miss
ISBN 978-3-7408-1107-5

Ed Glinert, Marc Zakian
111 Places in London's East End
That You Shouldn't Miss
ISBN 978-3-7408-0752-8

Nicola Perry, Daniel Reiter
33 Walks in London
That You Shouldn't Miss
ISBN 978-3-7408-1955-2

PHOTO CREDITS

All Star Lanes (ch. 2): All Star Lanes; Babylon Park (ch. 4): Babylon Park, London; Barking Park (ch. 5): Splash & Boats Ltd; The BMX Track London (ch. 8): Zakaria Yesema; Brixton Windmill (ch. 10): Courtesey of Friends of Windmill Gardens; Coal Drops Yard (ch. 19): John Sturrock c/o King's Cross; Discover Children's Story Centre (ch. 24): Discover Children's Story Centre; Elephant Springs (ch. 26): Lendlease, 2023; Gabriels Wharf (ch. 32): Coin Street; The Garden Museum (ch. 33): Garden Museum; Go Ape (ch. 35): Adventure Forest Ltd T/A Go Ape; GoBoat Paddington (ch. 36): GoBoat London; Headstone Manor (ch. 41): Headstone Manor & Museum; Hunterian Museum (ch. 42): Hufton and Crow by permission of Royal College of Surgeons of England; Kidspace Romford (ch. 46): Escapade Group; London Museum Docklands (ch. 51): London Museum; London Transport Museum (ch. 52): London Transport Museum; London Zoo (ch. 53): ZSL; The Old Operating Theatre Museum (ch. 66): The Old Operating Theatre Museum & Herb Garret, Southwark, London; Parsloes Park Play Area (ch. 67): Thierry Bal; The Postal Museum (ch. 71): The Postal Museum; Puppet Theatre Barge (ch. 72): Antonio Escalante and Alex Krook; The Royal Exchange (ch. 75): The Royal Exchange; The Sherriff Centre (ch. 78): The Sheriff Centre; Syon House and Park (ch. 88): Syon Park; Thames Rockets (ch. 93): Thames Rockets; Tower Bridge (ch. 97): Courtesy of Tower Bridge/City Bridge Foundation; Treasure Trails (ch. 98): Treasure Trails; Trinity Bouy Wharf (ch. 99): Trinity Bouy Wharf; Two Temple Place (ch. 100): Louis Berk, Two Temple Place, 2023; The Viktor Wynd Museum (ch. 103): Oskar Proctor; Walthamstow Pumphouse Museum (ch. 104): Walthamstow Pumphouse Museum

ACKNOWLEDGEMENTS

To my partner, who didn't complain (much) about our count-less London escapades, always managed to find the nearest coffee shop, and chased after our little explorer as I tried to take photos or gather information.

To my daughter, whose endless curiosity and bound-less energy turned every outing into a memorable adven-ture, even if it meant we often returned home with overpriced souvenirs as a thank you for her being the world's most enthusiastic camera assistant.

And to our dog, who wagged her tail through it all, ensuring every park was properly sniffed and every other dog was enthusiastically greeted.

Thank you all for being my partners-in-crime and for solidifying that the best way to rediscover London is together (even if it means frequent snack and toilet breaks!).

A special thank you to my grandmother. Nan, I am nothing with-out you. Thank you for everything.

Finally, it takes a village as they say, so of course putting together a book of this much content requires an extended special thanks to the following super stars:

Isaiah at All Star Lanes; Candice from Battersea Power Station; Ciara from Bow Street Police Museum; Catherine at Brixton Wind-mill Community Centre; Malaica from Coal Drops Yard; Melody from Coin Street; Rob at Crossness Engines Trust; Jess at Discover Children's Story Centre; Eddie at Elephant Springs; Beth from the Garden Museum; Victoria at GoBoat; Mat at God's Own Junkyard; Rachel at The Golden Hinde; Nathalie and Deborah of Fair Play Barnet; Mital at Go Ape; Sara from Headstone Manor; Graeme at Historic Croydon Airport Trust; Jessica from Kidspace Romford; Sam at Leake Street Arches; Alex at Lewis of London; Mariam at

London Museum Docklands; Alex from London Zoo; Candice at London Transport Museum; Nick from The Ludoquist; Kim and Rosie at Mayfield Lavender Farm; Bhavik from Neasden Temple; Monica at The Old Operating Theatre Museum; Zakaria at Peckham BMX; Tom at Postal Museum; Stan aboard The Puppet Theatre Barge; Bex at Royal College of Surgeons of England; Mie at The Sheriff Centre; Monika from Splash Park Barking; Sophie and Jess from Streatham Ice and Leisure Centre; Sarah at Syon Park; Georgie and Izzy from Thames Rockets; Katie and Georgia from Tower Bridge; Jonathan at Transpora Group; Alex from Treasure Trails; Patrycja from Trinity Buoy Wharf; Gabriella at Two Temple Place; Victoria at Walthamstow Pumphouse Museum, Ollie at Walthamstow Wetlands; and Hardip from Valentines Mansion.

And of course, the excellent Ros Horton, my editor, whom I only wish I had known when writing my dissertation! Thank you all, along with the brilliant team at Emons, for being part of the journey and helping to bring the book to life.

Alicia Edwards was born opposite Big Ben, and London has always been home. Spending countless mornings walking the streets of Central London with her grandad, growing up she grew to learn every inch of the West End and its secret backstreets and shortcuts. She'd also often jump on buses with her nan to explore the outer zones. Her love for the capital has never waned, as London never remains the same; there is always something new to find and explore. Since having a child of her own, Alicia has rediscovered London in a whole new light and loves it even more!